Thinking of...

Maximising your Investment as a Microsoft Partner?

Ask the Smart Questions

By Julie Simpson and Andy Trish

Smart Questions™ Philosophy

Smart Questions is built on 4 key pillars, which set it apart from other publishers:

1. *Smart people want Smart Questions not Dumb Answers*
2. *Domain experts are often excluded from authorship, so we are making writing a book simple and painless*
3. *The community has a great deal to contribute to enhance the content*
4. *We donate a percentage of revenue to a charity voted for by the authors and community. It is great marketing, but it is also the right thing to do*

www.Smart-Questions.com

What partners are saying

David Irwin,

Solutions Architect,

Ergo Computing

(Gold Certified Partner)

> *The CSAT can be a really powerful tool for assessing performance and customer opinion. If used correctly it will really benefit you rather than being a "tick in the box".*

> *Keep talking at least on a weekly basis with your account manager about your business wins and about your wishes, he/she will be able to direct you to the right person/programme.*

Philippe Limantour,

Managing Director,

YouSaaS,

(Gold Certified Partner)

> *The segmentation and metrics have changed for FY10 (this fiscal year). Understand them completely, find the most relevant areas that positively affect your business and then utilise your account manager to drive field integration strategies and awareness.*

Chris Teets, General Manager, Azaleos (Gold Certified Partner)

> *The internal use of licensing for production use and demos is really important. Not only to get the technical experience in using the latest products but to have sales confidence and realistic expectations of what the products do.*

Liam O'Mahony, Director, Computer Talk Ltd (Certified Partner)

Doug Tutus, CEO,

Newlease (Gold Certified Partner)

> *Work with an Account Manager on a business plan gaining commitment on the gives and gets.*

> *To obtain increased market share in Dynamics, Microsoft and its partners will need to take an approach that requires specialisation rather than generalisation.*

Garth D. Laird, President, ZAP (Gold Certified Partner)

Paul Doherty,

Sales & Marketing Director,

7Global

(Gold Certified Partner)

If I had to give one piece of advice it would be 'make use of what's on offer'. As a Microsoft partner you have access to £,£,£,s worth of resources your business can make use of.

As a startup the use of licenses and the Microsoft facilities are one of the major benefits and should be used from day one. Do whatever you can to attend the partner networking events.

Anders Trolle-Schultz,

Partner, SaaS-it Consult

(Registered Partner)

Will Saville,

Managing Director,

Brightstarr Ltd

(Gold Certified Partner)

I think it starts with being innovative - Taking Microsoft products and delivering creative and innovative solutions that demonstrate high return on investment.

Microsoft is built around partnership, ignore that simple fact and the consequences are obvious.

Ben Gower, Managing Director, Perspicuity Ltd (Gold Certified Partner)

Microsoft won't make you rich but your ability to capitalise on a quality Microsoft partnership may well do.

Jerome Mohamed,

Sales & Marketing Director, OctaviaIS (Gold Certified Partner)

We were a registered partner for four years. We decided to go for Gold and achieved it in 15 months. Why on earth did we wait four years

Ian Gotts, Founder and CEO, Nimbus Partners (Gold Certified Partner)

Authors

Julie Simpson

With over twenty years sales experience in a multitude of industries, Julie is the creator and Managing Director of ResourceiT Consulting Ltd, the unique organisation that provides end to end sales and marketing services only to Microsoft and its channel partners. ResourceiT has delivered over three hundred successful sales and marketing projects over the last five years with Microsoft partners of all shapes and sizes from small Independent Software Vendors, to large Enterprise partners.

Well known and respected for her straight talking and honest approach to business and as a source of insight and innovation for many Microsoft partners, keen to develop a more strategic relationship with Microsoft. Julie has written and presented at a plethora of Microsoft partner events in the UK and Europe. She is also the founder and author of MAD (the Microsoft Abbreviation Dictionary).

Andy Trish

Founding director of NCI Technologies, whose business is focused on providing the best IT Infrastructure solutions to small and medium enterprises. He achieved finalist status for the Advanced Infrastructure category, in the global partner awards at the Microsoft Worldwide Partner Conference in his second year of trading.

He was also awarded Microsoft Most Valuable Professional status and Partner Area Lead for Small Business Server in 2009 and is author of *Building your Small Business selling Microsoft Windows Small Business Server*. Andy has presented at many Microsoft Conferences and events.

Contributor

Emma Richardson

 Emma is the UK Partner Network Manager at Microsoft. Having worked on the Microsoft Partner Programme for the last four years, Emma knows the programme inside and out and is passionate about helping partners get the most from their membership. Emma is responsible for understanding the needs and feedback of Microsoft partners and ensuring that the programme develops and services those needs. This includes designing and launching the new Microsoft Partner Network for UK partners and customers. In addition, Emma is responsible for building and fostering the partner eco-system to ensure we have the right partners, with the right skills, delivering the right solutions to our customers.

An Introduction for Partners, by Julie Simpson and Andy Trish

A cynical bunch

As Microsoft partners we are a cynical bunch. There's an internal view of working with Microsoft, and then there's our view as partners - reality.

What we are is Microsoft's sales force – and sometimes we feel that Microsoft forgets that and bombards us with the information they want us to have, rather than the information we really need to grow our businesses.

We consistently get frustrated that we can't get answers to what seem to us quite straightforward questions – so much seems to be wrapped up in red tape. Why can't I get customer lists? Why won't you share with me the deals you are working on? Why won't you tell me what's in SharePoint 2010? Why indeed?

We work hard to identify the right individuals at Microsoft to work with – only to find they play musical jobs every six months and we then go through the whole cycle again, re-telling everything we have already said (at least five times before). Then there's the language! Where else would you find thousands of acronyms and abbreviations that we don't know or understand and seem to increase in volume on a weekly basis?

Decisions are made "at the great mother ship" in Redmond that are then pushed down to us mere mortals to implement. Leaving us feeling like there has been no consideration on the impact to our individual businesses.

We see the same partners over and over again being held up as examples of how we should run our businesses – when we feel that we can do a much better job.

Microsoft asks us to share our pipeline – share my pipeline?? You must be joking! What, so others can find out about my opportunities and engage directly? I don't think so.

New versions of software are produced so fast we have real troubling keeping up and yet we have to learn it to remain ahead and substantiate our claims of being experts in Microsoft technology.

So, why then do we still do it?

Our businesses are based around the Microsoft technologies, there is a huge customer base and despite our frustrations and cynicism there is money to be made. So we come to the conclusion that the only thing we can do to maximise our investment is to invest even further and dedicate resources with their associated costs to manage the relationship. We spend significant time networking ("hob knobbing") within the Microsoft business to build the right relationships. What does THAT cost our business – is the income going to be worth the investment?

We simply don't know – until we try.

When Microsoft invited us to write this book (alongside their input of course) we did wonder what the content would end up like. How much could we get on these pages that was a partner's view of life and how much would be Microsoft's?

Suffice to say this has ended up as a bit of both. What we have tried to produce is a view of what being a Microsoft partner really means and all the things you can do to maximise your investment in that partnership. A lot of the things we are recommending in this book are about how you view your own business and to be honest, a bit of a reality check on what should be happening whether you are a Microsoft partner, Oracle partner, florist, retailer or plumber. Some things are just good business practice and if we all put more of them in place we would most definitely achieve much greater things, much quicker.

We are all very similar companies and we all have the same advantages and opportunities. How is it then that some companies grow and develop much quicker than others? Why do some partners always seem to land on their feet when they take what appear to be high risks on new products or solutions which then turn out to be "best sellers" (early adopters of SharePoint for example)?

Maybe it's not just luck. Maybe it's something else...

Our journey has led us into many different areas of the partner programme. Some of the benefits and resources we knew were there but hadn't really stopped to explore in detail – and some we just simply weren't aware of. What we can tell you is that the resources Microsoft make available to partners are vast, however there really are huge areas of the programme that are seriously under-utilised by partners. What has become blatantly obvious to us (and we hope will become blatantly obvious to you) is that having made the decision to "bet your business" (or at least a portion of it) on Microsoft – are you really utilising all of the benefits associated with that decision?

Microsoft sells its products and services through a third party channel – us. It produces a programme that contains a substantial amount of resources we could use to run our businesses more efficiently from technical to marketing and from business to sales. So as well as what we consider to be some sound business advice, we have also included some of the key features of what is now the Microsoft Partner Network and then asked Microsoft to contribute to it – just to make sure we are getting our facts absolutely right.

We hope this is a good read for you. We hope that you get to the end, feeling you now know a wee bit more about the resources Microsoft has created to supports its sales channel and more than that can see how you could use them in your business. Don't be surprised if it suddenly occurs to you as you read through this that you are spending cash you don't need to – cash that could be invested elsewhere, or may even bring that villa in the sun much closer to you than you would consider was possible.

We also sincerely hope we have dispelled some of the myths, given some insider insight that is based on years of working with Microsoft and have provided you with something that will be a valuable tool for you to "Maximise your Investment as a Microsoft partner". If everyone that reads this takes away one thing that increases revenue for their business then we have done our job.

For you to decide read on...

Table of Contents

Acknowledgements

To all the partners who, whether knowingly or not, have provided the experiences that have allowed this book to be written.

Foreword

"How exactly do I get more from my relationship with Microsoft?" A question I often get asked when I'm out talking to partners. Working in a large, global organisation, many of us often forget how challenging it can be to know where to start your relationship. A relationship with Microsoft isn't just about the personal, face to face engagement. It helps – but it's not the only resource available.

Seven years ago, the Microsoft Partner Programme was first introduced into the channel. It's grown and adapted into something quite different from the original. Partners and customers provide daily feedback on what works and what doesn't and this has helped us build an industry leading partner channel.

At Microsoft, more than any other time in our history, we have a product line that allows small and large partners opportunities to sell, develop and integrate complete solutions for their customers.

Why a network? Delivering on customer needs is central to success, so Microsoft and its partners need a customer-centric approach. Customers want to work with the "best" partner – who is innovative, and drives value for the customer. Working together, we can ensure that the Microsoft Partner Network is a brand and quality bar that's valued by our customers – and then we all win.

The Microsoft Partner Network is all about connections. We want to help you make connections with and through the Microsoft Partner Network. I encourage you to learn about the wealth of benefits available to you and your company – use them to gain the best advantage.

I was delighted to hear this book was being written by partners for partners. I believe that using this book across your business will help you make the connections and customer opportunities that you need for success. That's good news for all of us.

Scott Dodds (General Manager for Small and Midmarket Solutions and Partners Group, Microsoft Ltd)

Who should read this book?

People like you and me

This book is intended to help you get the most out of your partnership with Microsoft. We trust it will be a catalyst for action aimed at a range of people inside and outside your organisation. Here are just a few, and why it is relevant to them.

Chief Executive Officer/Owner

Whether you are on your own or have a team of staff under you, the future of your company is on your shoulders. If you take time out to read this book you will re-evaluate how you can grow your company with Microsoft

Partner Manager/Microsoft Alliance Manager

Your job is managing the relationship with Microsoft. This book is a no-brainer for you. It will help you understand Microsoft better and give you ideas about how to deepen your relationship, to ensure that you get what you need from the partnership.

Sales and Marketing Director

You have a budget and you have an objective. Your budget is probably already stretched – and you are under considerable pressure to get ahead in what is now a very tough and competitive market - now is the time to look at what resources are available to you as a partner that will save you time and money. You'll probably find there are activities that you're currently paying for that you can actually get for free as a partner.

Chief Operating Officer

The daily operations of your business are your utmost importance. Streamlining your processes and making your staff efficient are an important part of your role. Here we will help you maximise the tools available to you as a Microsoft partner, achieving the required results in less time, with less cost.

Chief Information Officer/Chief Technical Officer

A skilled, trained workforce can dramatically improve bottom line performance, adding value to products and services and making it easier to compete. Satisfied and motivated workers mean higher levels of staff retention, lowering the costs of recruitment. We guide your thoughts on certification and training as a means to success in business, providing quality work and great customer service

How to use this book

This book is intended to be the catalyst for action. We hope that the ideas and examples inspire you to act. So, do whatever you need to do to make this book useful. Use Post-it notes, photocopy pages, scan pages, and write on it. Rip it apart, or read it quickly in one sitting. Whatever works for you. We hope this becomes your most dog-eared book.

Getting Involved

Send us your feedback

We love feedback. We prefer great reviews, but we'll accept anything that helps take the ideas further. There may be questions that we should have asked but didn't. Or specific questions which may be relevant to your situation, but not everyone in general. This is a key part of the Smart Questions Philosophy so please send us your comments. You never know, they may make it into the next edition of the book.

We'd prefer email, as it's easy to answer and saves trees. If the ideas worked for you, we'd love to hear your success stories. Maybe we could turn them into 'Talking Heads'-style video or audio interviews on our website, so others can learn from you. That's one of the reasons why we wrote this book. So talk to us.

feedback@Smart-Questions.com

Got a book you need to write?

Maybe you are a domain expert with knowledge locked up inside you. You'd love to share it and there are people out there desperate for your insights. But you don't think you are an author and don't know where to start. Making it easy for you to write a book is part of the Smart Questions Philosophy.

Let us know about your book idea, and let's see if we can help you get your name in print.

potentialauthor@Smart-Questions.com

Chapter

Opportunity everywhere

Luck is what happens when preparation meets opportunity.

Seneca (Roman Philosopher, mid-1st century AD)

Decisions, Decisions

THE very first thing you need to ask yourself when making a choice to partner with a supplier, vendor or another partner is what is in it for you, after all, you are in business to make money.

In this book we are talking about how to benefit from your relationship with a specific company, Microsoft. Your relationship starts with a membership in the Microsoft Partner Network, but this is just the tip of the Microsoft iceberg. Before we get into this, the first thing you need understand is why you want to partner with

Microsoft and whether you can gain the momentum as the relationship flourishes.

It really doesn't matter if you are a sole trader or a corporate institution, the motivational reasons for any partnership can determine the success or failure of the outcome.

As an organisation Microsoft has become one of the global mega-brands and it can be quite daunting to think they actually want to help you grow your company. But as with any good partnership, it's a two way street. Experience tells us that you can get so much more out of a successful business partnership if you focus on where you want to be over a defined time.

Whether you are a sole trader or a big corporation, it is important to understand that the more you want any partnership to succeed, the more you need to invest. You can simply pay a fee and get back the basics that your partner level offers or you can give freely, show willing and reap the benefits.

Prospects galore

In the current financial climate there are many businesses suffering, many through no fault of their own. Banks withdrawing funding needed for specific projects, customers attempting to extend credit terms or simply not spending until they see a brighter future, but it's not all gloomy.

This is the time to evaluate your business plans and decide where to head your company in the future. Have a look out of your window - who supports all the offices around you and where do they buy their hardware? Are they using your software and, if not, would it improve the way they work?

There are many business owners and managers out there who would jump at the opportunity of getting good support or software development or any of the great things Microsoft partners do, the main problem is getting your foot in the door and letting them know you exist.

Exploiting new opportunities

Striking the right balance between delivering a good service for your existing customers and developing your business to take advantage of new market opportunities is a real challenge. The last thing you want to do is expose your "bread and butter" business by not staying focused on what you do well. But in order to retain competitive edge you must continue to mature and develop your business, keep alert about new market opportunities as they arise, and move fast to take advantage of them.

The question is how do you make the right decisions about which new markets, solution areas or products to pursue?

Microsoft has to continually drive partners to pick up new technologies and stay up to date with the latest versions of software if it is to maintain its market leading position and recoup its consistent and substantial investment in R &D. What is not productive, however, is when partners invest time and energy into getting to grips with a new product or solution that is so far out of their core area of expertise, that their existing customer base will not buy it.

The most successful partners think carefully and logically about which products and solutions they stay up to date with. They make sure that throughout their businesses all staff are consistently staying up to date. Technologists attend events, webinars and online tutorials. Marketing people research the relevant vertical markets and keep ahead with Microsoft's market penetration strategies. Sales people make sure they are aware of and are using all the pre-sales tools available and are up to date with the key sales messages associated.

Once early awareness is released by Microsoft, these partners also start asking questions within their existing customers and begin to provide thought leadership and advice about how their customers can gain competitive edge by being early adopters of the technology. Because Microsoft is also keen to drive adoption, it will proactively approach the partners it thinks are best positioned to create early hype in the market and will help to get the stuff out there. It is important that you are focused and gain recognition as an expert if you want to exploit this opportunity to its maximum and get on the right lists with Microsoft.

My life as a Microsoft Channel Alliance Manager, by Julie Simpson

In a previous life as the Microsoft Alliance Manager for an IT company, my Managing Director said to me: "Julie, there are other partners out there eating our lunch, what are you going to do about it?"

I was working alongside the MD to enhance and develop our profile with Microsoft as well as being an active member of the sales and management team. This was hugely varied and definitely meant I did a different job every day.

In the beginning, I kind of felt Microsoft owed me something – we were a Gold partner after all, committed to the programme, selling solutions based on the platform, attending events and generally reasonably active in the channel. Why don't I get sales leads? Why wasn't Microsoft paying for our marketing? I really didn't know what I didn't know - my MD's view? "You've got no relationships" – was he right at that time? Probably.

I knew I needed to get to the bottom of this by understanding how the partner business model worked and what I could realistically expect in terms of direct Microsoft support. I certainly knew there were other partners out there doing a much better job than I was of building a consistent and valuable relationship both with Microsoft and with other partners (and seeing the value from it). But I really didn't know where to begin.

As always for me, a plan seemed like a good idea. I wrote a list of things I needed to find out, and then some ideas about where and who I could get the answers from.

As any good sales person would, the first thing was to start with some research and get myself some facts, so I started digging.

First stop – Microsoft partner portal. On entry I went straight to the case studies. I wasn't looking to see what the customer solutions were, I was looking to see who the partners were that had case studies on the Microsoft website in our solution areas. My thinking was, if these partners are getting their solutions published, Microsoft must know who they are.

Bingo. It didn't take long before I had a list of partners that were competing with us not only with customers, but who also clearly had a closer relationship with Microsoft than I did. I should mention at this point that this was several years ago, when the partner programme and portal were much smaller than they are today, with information much more accessible - and there was a lot less of it!

Armed with my list (which was only about fifteen companies) I went individually to their websites and profiled each organisation.

By the sixth one, I could see exactly what was different. They were clear about what they did, what they could deliver, and were clearly communicating that – and I wasn't.

Next stop, our techies. We had some amazing technical people in the business who were always presenting at Microsoft. A few had worked there in the past and clearly had some great relationships (unlike myself). This time was so well spent - "I use this area of the site to find out information on the latest software which helps me do my job, this guy runs it"; "I have this community I talk to about stuff and share ideas, there's a bunch of us involved and we meet up sometimes"; "I always go to events where this guy is presenting, he really knows his stuff and he really enjoys my questions and interaction. I email him from time to time when I am stuck with something".

Right.

Back to the portal with fresh eyes – keen to see what I could find out in terms of marketing benefits, tools and places to get ourselves out there. It wasn't long before I came up with a few templates to download and complete on our solutions, some campaign messaging, aligned to our own customer campaigns and a list of events to attend (relevant to me in my role and to my company).

And then there was light...

What became very obvious was that success here was going to be about mutual benefit. Not just what Microsoft could do for us, but what we could also do for Microsoft.

Within a couple of weeks I went back to my MD with a plan. He was really quite impressed (even though praise was not his strongest attribute). After some internal brainstorming we had some great ideas on how we could raise our profile and begin on a much more structured journey with Microsoft which had the potential to considerably accelerate our business growth.

We built use of the Microsoft programme tools and resources fully into my area of the business. We made sure we were signed up and utilising all the available assets and soon got a reputation within Microsoft for being "an active partner".

The fact is, once I began to use my little grey cells, asked some sensible questions, got to know the benefits and resources available through the programme and thought about the message and value I was communicating, and then identified the people that would care about what we did, my relationship was transformed.

When we held our Christmas party both my MD and I used our personal relationships to invite a bunch of people from Microsoft to come along and celebrate with us. I had to smile when all of my invitees came to the party, but none of those my MD had invited could make it.

"So, now who hasn't got any relationships"? **(Julie Simpson)**

My life as a Microsoft Gold Certified partner, by Andy Trish

Taking the first steps in any relationship is difficult, especially when you are offered a choice of commitment and a fee may be involved.

A few years ago as a computer engineer working for another company I was always looking at ways to make the company more profitable even though it wasn't a part of my job. The company I worked for had a staff base of twenty five and were heavily involved with HP as a partner but hadn't even considered Microsoft, after all what could Microsoft bring to the table to a company whose primary focus was getting boxes out of the door?

Microsoft had recently formed the Microsoft Partner Programme (MSPP) and partnering with them was an unknown to us. You wouldn't believe the pain I had to go through to get my boss to part with his money, it was such a challenge that I nearly volunteered to pay for it myself.

Almost immediately after signing up to the programme the engineers were solving problems much quicker. Critical issues that in the past had taken up so many internal resources could be solved so much quicker and just the fact that our sales people could advertise the fact we were a Microsoft partner increased business.

The year after that, my boss rushed down to see me and ask if I had renewed yet, his comment when I asked about the fee was "we can't afford not to".

Times move on and I started my own company bringing with me some colleagues. Because I already knew the value others had gained from being a Microsoft partner one of my first moves was to sign up and invest time in moving quickly up the tier system in order to take advantage of the most amount of benefits available to me

Year one of business was tough, I'm not kidding when I say twenty one hour days were the norm but if I hadn't taken the step to partner with Microsoft, to the level I had, I can honestly say my business wouldn't be where it is today.

Walking into a potential customer the other day I was asked if there was a way for them to get staff to have notification of events happening within the company and a holiday calendar. I was told the budget would be found if I came up with the right solution. They already had Small Business Server and were amazed when I spent ten minutes showing them some of the features built in to their company intranet and that SharePoint was the solution they already owned.

For them it was an easy choice, a stranger had come in and solved their needs in just ten minutes by showing them something that had been installed years ago but the company who installed it simply never showed them what it did. No matter how good a service their previous IT Company had given them, their flaw was not giving that little bit extra. I walked away with a twelve month premium support contract and an order for new hardware and configuration of their SharePoint. The bite in this tale is my company doesn't have the skills to configure SharePoint. However, by being a member of the Microsoft Partner Network and taking advantage of the benefits available, such as Channel Builder, I was able to find another Microsoft partner to do the SharePoint work and we both ended up with a happy customer.

It may take a bit of time to get your head around some of the tools and resources in the Microsoft Partner Network, but they can make all the difference when it comes to collaborating, selling, marketing or training your staff and customers

Different steps for different people, all are good and all can achieve great things but if you don't take that first step you'll never move up the ladder. **(Andy Trish)**

Getting your staff on board

It doesn't matter if the times are tough or work is in abundance, having good staff dedicated to the success of the company can make the difference on each and every opportunity.

It's how you utilise those staff that puts you on the podium of great business people. Not every business can afford to dedicate one role to each employee, in fact many employees not only have multiple roles but those roles change as needs require.

Once you have decided to make a commitment to partner with Microsoft you need to let your staff know, and express to them what it will mean to your company both now and in the future.

Don't be scared of showing them what your company gets in the way of material, training or resources. You can't take this road alone if you want your company to stand out. It's amazing the ideas that are presented by staff when they see the marketing resources, sales information and technical tools available to them.

Doing the right thing

Just because you can, it doesn't mean you should. There are many factors to consider when you are offered a "partner" opportunity that will require you to commit time and resources. It may appear attractive, but as Microsoft partners, we are only too aware that there may be obstacles in the way of a successful outcome.

The more you commit, the heavier the load on resources. Each department within Microsoft is run as its own business, within a business. Ultimately each department does align to the same goals, primarily tied to generating revenue and developing customer and partner satisfaction with Microsoft. But when you work with them it can seem like they all have a different agenda. It can be difficult, the more you get involved, to manage your time and focus on the things that matter to you – YOUR business.

Why Microsoft and not someone else?

The focus of this book is the Microsoft Partner Network. But there are of course other vendors and they have their own programs. If you have skills in their offerings and you can gain value from their membership programme then go ahead and join. Our word of caution would be that depending on the size of your business you may have to consider whether you have the resources to effectively maintain multiple partner relationships. To achieve more than simply having a vendor logo on your web site takes a real commitment.

But why should you consider Microsoft as the place where you make that partner commitment? To answer that question, we must first acknowledge that Microsoft is a software company that invests over $8 billion per year in research and development. It exists to produce software. Always has and probably always will. Additionally, 96% of Microsoft's revenue is generated by partners. It is totally unique in that it is the only software vendor that (more or less) sells its products through third parties. Put simply, partners are Microsoft's route to market and they take partnering very seriously.

The following is an extract from materials describing the Microsoft Partner Network. Microsoft has to deliver on this vision and promise, but it clearly shows their intent.

Microsoft's Vision and Promise

The Microsoft Partner Network is a community born from Microsoft's continued commitment to serve the needs of their partners and help them reach their full potential.

The vision for the Partner Network is simple —

- To provide opportunities for partners to develop and expand their business.

- To provide expertise and resources that help partners better serve their customers.

- To create passionate communities that spark innovation by connecting partners with one another.

Working together, Microsoft continue to focus on creating innovative solutions that drive profitability and sustain competitive advantage.

And if you can handle the more "creative" language used by the people who design logos, you may be interested to hear what the new Microsoft Partner Network logo represents:

The Microsoft Partner Network logo

"Inspired by the metaphor of a nest and rooted in the belief that the strongest nest yields the greatest wings of opportunity, our logo is a dynamic, vibrant, and multidimensional visualisation of our business network and the opportunities that network presents for us and our partners. Speaking to our shared future, the nest represents both the relationships we have with our partners, as well as those that they have with one another."

"Three triangles intertwining with one another create an integrated, singular whole that is both supportive and optimistic. Bright, transparent colours merge and vibrate, reflecting the energy of our network of partners and the dialogue between its members."

Microsoft Partner Network™

Microsoft made a decision from almost day one that they would have an indirect route to market. Industry experts suggest that this was one of the key factors that allowed Microsoft to grow so rapidly and reach the industry leading position it now occupies. With a huge and growing product portfolio the need for partners is even more essential. Even if Microsoft wanted to, it would be impossible to build out a services team that could provide the breadth and depth of skills, knowledge and resources needed to satisfy the millions of consumers and businesses that use Microsoft products.

Partners provide the connection between Microsoft products and the end customer's needs. This means that a partner has two relationships. With Microsoft it is all about understanding the new products as they arrive and working out how to use and innovate with them. We could call this an Innovation Relationship. The end customer however is interested in solving problems, whether they be business or consumer focused. The partner needs to demonstrate their skills to the customer through a Value Relationship. Understanding these two relationships is important in maximising your investment as a Microsoft partner.

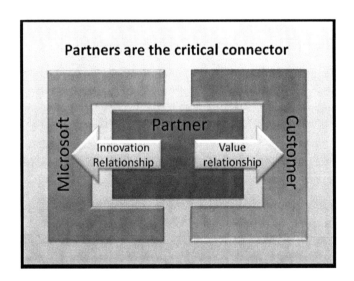

Getting involved early

Just by participating in the Microsoft Partner Network you have shown your commitment. Here we talk about ways to enhance your opportunities in both business development and software development by getting involved at an early stage of new product launches.

Partners participating and actively contributing to beta programmes is a key part of Microsoft's product development lifecycle. Being part of these provides early insight to the technologies and potentially competitive go-to-market opportunities for partners. But how do you get onto those programmes in the first place?

Because the range of products Microsoft develops is expanding so are the opportunities to get involved. For example all attendees at the Microsoft Worldwide Partner Conference (WPC) 2009 were invited on to the Office 2010 Technical Preview programme. There were no other requirements, no hoops to jump through; you simply had to be an attendee.

This isn't the case for all programmes. Microsoft understands that a lot of people want to experience their products before launch. However, even for Microsoft there are limited budgets and resources. Having 300,000 people all reporting bugs on a product with ten developers working on it isn't manageable.

There are many routes to finding out about these early adopter programmes, but as usual talking with your account manager is a good place to start. It is also well worth getting to know people within the Microsoft Developer and Platform Evangelism (DPE) team - their role in life, as the title suggests, is to evangelise about Microsoft's products as they come to market. If you want to be involved, just try asking.

There are a number of generic programmes that cover the early adopter stages e.g. Metro and TAP (Technical Adoption Programme). TAP is designed for partners to get real world customer feedback on Microsoft pre-release products. If you are doing great work in an area that Microsoft is developing new products in, then by letting them know, you may get invited to get involved as a TAP partner for that product.

If you develop products that work on or with Microsoft solutions, then you should be looking to get those products certified for Windows. This not only allows you access to the 'Certified for Windows' logo but adds value to your Competencies in the Microsoft Partner Network.

Microsoft regularly invites partners to shout about the solutions they have implemented for their customers and will publish Microsoft case studies showcasing the great work done by partners on behalf of their customers. This is especially true in the run up to a new product launch where Microsoft want to show that lots of partners are already on board and ready. Adding Microsoft case studies to your marketing portfolio can seriously enhance your image with other customers.

Opportunity everywhere

Chapter

Nothing stands still

The art of progress is to preserve order amid change and to preserve change amid order.

Alfred North Whitehead (Philosopher, 1861 – 1947)

YOU'VE got this far in the book so must have decided this is the right thing for you or, at the very least, still be considering how to make the next move.

This book is being written at an interesting time, because Microsoft has just announced the next generation of their membership programme, called the Microsoft Partner Network. This is the evolution of the existing membership programme, the Microsoft Partner Programme, which has been in existence for around seven years. And it hasn't changed much during that time, although the market has significantly changed. The new Partner Network has been designed based on your feedback, and according to Microsoft it is taking a "customer-centric approach – focussing on helping customers, partners and Microsoft "connect", and helping partners build their capability (skills) to service their customers better". Hence the use of the work Network in the name.

Although the membership programme is evolving, this doesn't affect how you should work with Microsoft or the questions you should be asking yourself as you grow your relationship. In fact, with this change comes the opportunity to reflect on how you are representing yourself to Microsoft and make changes to get the most from the membership.

Out with the old, in with the new

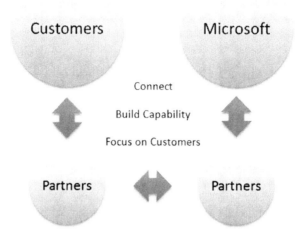

The Microsoft Partner Network focus areas: Connect, Capability, Customers

The previous Microsoft Partner Programme had a very formal structure – with three tier levels of membership (Registered, Certified, Gold) and a points system to achieve the top levels of membership (Certified and Gold). One of the methods of earning points was to earn a Competency – which is an area of specialisation earned by having technically skilled staff and evidence of customer projects delivered in that solution area. The problem with this system was that partners weren't choosing one area and specialising, instead, because the requirements were a bit too easy, partners were clocking up multiple Competencies regardless of whether they delivered work in this area. As a result, partners often came across as "Jack of all trades, master of none" and it became difficult for Microsoft to identify the partners with real expertise. This meant that partners didn't get the visibility and opportunities they had hoped for or their commitment deserved. The attitude became such that membership was simply a tick-box exercise, and no time was spent on understanding how to make best use of the programme.

 In essence, the Partner Programme had lost some of its value for Partners, customers and Microsoft, and it was time for a rethink.

In the new Microsoft Partner Network subscription model the tier system has been removed. So no more Certified and Gold. Instead of a tier system, there will be two different places you can land in the Partner Network – a partner with a Competency, and a partner without a Competency. Those in the latter bucket will have the option to be a Registered partner, or to become a partner with a subscription to one of our programmes aimed at smaller businesses – for example Microsoft Action Pack, Empower, BizSpark or WebsiteSpark. Your level of engagement with Microsoft will be dependent on where you land in the Partner Network subscription model.

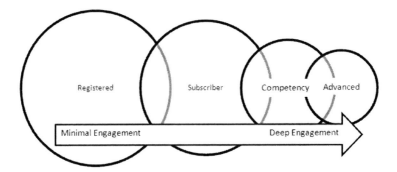

The Microsoft Partner Network subscription model

Before you panic about losing your Gold or Certified brand, let us explain Microsoft's rationale. As mentioned above, it started to become too easy to get to Gold membership – this meant that Microsoft ended up with too many Gold partners, and the Gold brand became diluted. This Gold brand was also very generic – it didn't make it obvious to a customer what the partner was 'gold' in, i.e. what solution area. So the Microsoft Partner Network doesn't run on a tier system, instead it runs on subscription and Competency model. In the Partner Network there are thirty Competencies which a partner can choose from to achieve. If a partner really wants to excel, you can then choose to achieve the 'Advanced' level within a Competency. This is a bit like becoming Gold in a Competency. So now you can go out to your customers and shout about being the best within that solution area.

When is this all happening?

Microsoft have learnt their lesson about changing things too quickly – so they're giving partners eighteen months to get comfortable with the changes. The changes were announced publicly in July 2009 at the Worldwide Partner Conference in New Orleans, and most of the changes won't happen until October 2010 and beyond.

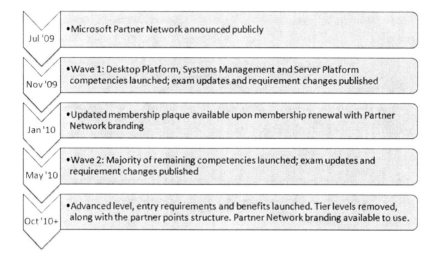

The Microsoft Partner Network roadmap

How does this impact me?

If you're already in the existing Partner Programme, you may be wondering how this change impacts your membership.

I'm a Gold partner...

As a Gold partner it's likely you already meet the requirements for a Competency at the standard level so you will probably find that your account is migrated to the new Competency. If you hold multiple Competencies, you will see some changes happening to the Competencies you hold. This is because Microsoft is moving from a model of having sixteen Competencies and forty-two specialisations (sub-Competencies), to having thirty Competencies. This list of thirty Competencies has been compiled by a) combining some of the original Competencies and specialisations into one new Competency; b) promoting some of the original specialisations to Competency status; c) creating brand new Competencies to cater for new types of partners e.g. web-site designers. Within each Competency you can work towards achieving an Advanced level to show that you are an expert in that solution area. As a result, you may find that today you have four Competencies and two specialisations, and in tomorrow's world you have two Competencies, of which one you choose to work towards achieving an Advanced level.

I'm a Certified partner...

You'll need to make a decision about where you want to be in the Partner Network. If you already have one Competency, then you can fulfil any additional requirements that are added and retain that Competency. Or you can look to move into the Advanced level within that Competency and significantly increase your exposure within Microsoft, and gain a stronger brand to take out to your customers. If you don't currently have a Competency, then you will become a Registered partner – so you have the option to either subscribe to one of the programmes aimed at smaller businesses, e.g. BizSpark or Action Pack, designed to help partners grow, or you can work towards a Competency.

I'm a Registered partner...

There's no impact for you – only opportunities. As a Registered partner you have the opportunity to either continue with your current level of engagement with Microsoft, or to step up a level and subscribe to one of the programmes designed to help grow your business. For example, Microsoft Action Pack provides Registered partners with software licences and sales resources; Empower offers Registered Independent Software Vendor partners with licences for development; BizSpark and WebsiteSpark provide resources to support start-up businesses. As you join these programmes, you will start to see more opportunities within Microsoft and your level of engagement will increase.

I'm an SBSC partner...

If you are currently a member of the Small Business Specialist Community (SBSC), there is a significant change for you – but it is a very positive change. There were a few challenges with the SBSC programme – namely that it didn't sit within the Partner Programme Competency structure, which meant that these partners didn't always receive the same benefits as partners with a Competency within the Partner Programme. Additionally the partners who achieved the SBSC status weren't necessarily the 'right' partners – there were a mixture of genuine partners who focussed on small businesses, partners who just wanted to earn extra points to get to Gold, and partners who were sole traders who just wanted the 'status' and couldn't get a brand identity in any other way (all Competencies required two or more employees).

In the Partner Network, Microsoft has now created two new Competencies – Small Business and Medium Business Solution Provider. Both of these have entry routes for sole traders, and are only for partners who focus on small to midsized businesses. Partners will be rewarded with a brand identity for earning the Competency, which is all part of the main Partner Network branding. Partners who sit in the SBSC programme will likely be migrated to the relevant Competency in October 2010, if they meet the entry requirements. Microsoft is then committing to drive the Partner Network brand heavily to customers, to replace the current SBSC brand that partners were using.

How does achieving an Advanced Competency really help me?

The introduction of an Advanced level is Microsoft's way of recognising that all of our businesses are different. Advanced applies to a specific solution Competency so you can be Advanced in a Competency that your company really concentrates its efforts on and standard in another which is great for partners and customers alike. If you have a company that specialises in server platform solutions but also deal in licensing, you may have achieved Competencies in both but be Advanced in one and standard in the other. This makes it really clear to a customer where your expertise sits.

This also adds more value to Microsoft because the partners who meet the tough requirements to achieve the Advanced level will be the top partners who they want to engage with. And with thirty Competencies to choose from, there are sure to be many of the existing Gold partners aiming their sights on achieving at least one Advanced Competency. The worry here, of course, is that the requirements would be made too easy for obtaining Advanced, and the status would become diluted as happened with Gold. However, the initial requirements announced by Microsoft sound quite tough. Currently the requirements look to be tied to high levels of technical expertise, customer satisfaction and commitment to Microsoft. This time around Microsoft are promising to be strict with these requirements - no partners will be exempt or will get 'special case' treatment. The message from the 2009 Worldwide Partner Conference was that Microsoft are looking to partners to commit to their technology and to prove their worth as a partner, achieving an Advanced level is a great way to do this. This strong message is being delivered not just for the Partner Network, but for any partners working on competitive technology – now is the time that Microsoft are looking for partners to make the choice, and partners who make this commitment will get a higher chance of exposure and opportunity within the product groups.

What are the new Competencies?

There are thirty Competencies in the Microsoft Partner Network, which partners can work to achieve from October 2010. Each Competency will have a standard level and an Advanced level. This Competency model consists of some original Competencies and some brand new Competencies.

Application Integration	Application Lifecycle Management	Authorised Distributor	Business Intelligence	Content Management	Customer Relationship Management
Data Platform	Desktop Platform	Digital Home	Digital Marketing	Enterprise Resource Planning	Hosting Platform
Identity and Security	ISV/Software	Learning	Medium Business Solution Provider	Mobility	OEM Hardware
Portals and Collaboration	Project and Portfolio Management	Search	Server Platform	Small Business	Software Asset Management
Software Development	Systems Management	Unified Comms	Virtualisation	Volume Licensing	Web Development

The Microsoft Partner Network Competency structure

How will industries be included in this?

The Microsoft Partner Programme has never really provided opportunities for partners to identify themselves as working in a particular vertical industry. The Partner Network, however, is likely to bring improvements to the way it provides industry focus. This is likely to include new communities such as the Education Community. More detail on this is likely to be made available on this in 2010.

What if I want to become Gold today or renew my current status?

There is a transition period between retiring the Partner Programme and launching the Partner Network. If you want to move up from Registered and Certified to Gold or you want to renew your membership between now and October 2010, you should do this using the existing Partner Programme membership rules. This means you will need to earn the partner points to qualify, associate your MCPs and customer references, and process payment on the partner portal. In addition, Gold partners will need to use the CSAT survey tool to measure their customers' satisfaction as part of the renewal process. Gold partners will need to use the tool in the previous twelve months prior to their renewal date to qualify for Gold. This was a new requirement introduced in October 2009 which was introduced to support the message of the Partner Network becoming more customer-centric. From October 2010, the tier structure and the partner points structure will be removed, the new logo introduced for partners to use, and new competency requirements will be introduced which you will need to follow to establish yourself in the programme, or to renew your membership.

What if I'm a Registered partner today and I want to 'grow' in the Partner Network?

As mentioned above, there is a transition period. If you are looking to 'grow' within the Partner Network, you should continue to do so by either joining one of the specific programmes, such as Action Pack, Empower, BizSpark or WebsiteSpark, or by gaining the certifications to achieve Certified level. Any time and effort spent skilling your staff on the latest technology won't be wasted – the certification requirements for the new Competencies will be based on the latest technology.

So what is all of this going to cost me?

As this book is written we are not aware of any changes in the membership – the announcement made at the Worldwide Partner Conference 2009 was that the membership fee would remain at £1,050 per year. However, the smart business person will understand it's not just about the membership fee. There are hidden costs with the time and effort it takes to fully understand the membership programme and swim through all the resources to find the ones that will help you.

 Microsoft aren't making a profit on your membership fee – they run the Partner Network as an investment with partners, and any money generated is spent on developing the programme benefits.

Chapter

Ask the Smart Questions

If I have seen further it is by standing on the shoulders of giants

Isaac Newton (Scientist, 1643 – 1727)

S MART Questions is about giving you valuable insights or "the Smarts". Normally these are only gained through years of painful and costly experience. Whether you already have a general understanding of the subject and need to take it to the next level or are starting from scratch, you need to make sure you ask the Smart Questions. We aim to short circuit that learning process, by providing the expertise of the 'giants' that Isaac Newton referred to.

Not all the questions will necessarily be new or staggeringly insightful. The value you get from the information will clearly vary. It depends on your job role and previous experience. We call this the 3Rs.

The 3 Rs

Some of the questions will be in areas where you know all the answers so they will be **Reinforced** in your mind.

You may have forgotten certain areas so the book will **Remind** you.

And other questions may be things you've never considered and will be **Revealed** to you.

How do you use Smart Questions?

The structure of the questions is set out in Chapter 4, and the questions are in Chapters 5, 6 and 7. The questions are laid out in a series of structured and ordered tables with the questions in one column and the explanation of why it matters alongside. We've also provided a checkbox so that you can mark which questions are relevant to your particular situation.

A quick scan down the first column in the list of questions should give you a general feel of where you are for each question vs. the 3Rs.

At the highest level they are a sanity check or checklist of areas to consider. You can take them with you to meetings or use them to stimulate your own ideas. Just one question may save you a whole heap of cash or heartache.

In Chapter 8 we've tried to bring some of the questions to life with some real-life examples. There may be some 'aha' moments. Hopefully not too many sickening, 'head in the hands – what have we done' moments. Even if you are in that situation, then the questions will help you negotiate yourself back into control.

In this context, probably the most critical role of the questions is that they reveal risks that you hadn't considered and opportunities you hadn't necessarily thought about. Balancing the opportunities and the risks, and then agreeing what is realistically achievable is the key to formulating a strategy.

How to dig deeper

Need more information? Not convinced by the examples, or want ones that are more relevant to you specific situation? We would encourage you to go to the Microsoft partner portal or contact the Ask Partner helpline or your account manager. There are also a list of websites and telephone numbers at the back of this book for all the resources mentioned.

And finally

Please remember that these questions are NOT intended to be a prescriptive list that must be followed slavishly from beginning to end. It is also inevitable that the list of questions is not exhaustive and we are confident that with the help of the community the list of Smart Questions will grow.

If you want to rephrase a question to improve its context or have identified a question we've missed, then let us know so we can add it to the collective knowledge.

We also understand that not all of the questions will apply to all businesses. However we encourage you to read them all as there may be a nugget of truth that can be adapted to your circumstances.

Above all we do hope that it provides a guide or a pointer to the areas that may be valuable to you and helps with the "3 Rs".

Chapter

The questions to ask

The important thing is not to stop questioning

Albert Einstein (Physicist, 1879 – 1955)

Y OUR business as a Microsoft partner is just that. It's *your* business – not Microsoft's. Your association with Microsoft is a part of it, but it is not the whole focus. What

you have chosen to do is make an investment in Microsoft as a strategic software vendor. You should be keen to achieve maximum profit from that decision. You cannot expect Microsoft to run your business for you, be wholly responsible for passing you new business leads or be held accountable if you make bad decisions about where you should focus your efforts and resources.

With 425,000 partners worldwide, and over 30,000 in the UK, Microsoft has to provide information about everything it does, to everyone that needs it – whatever their focus area. What you have to do is recognise which areas of the Partner Network are relevant to you – making sure you select the bits that will help to make you more profitable. With over 140 membership benefits, that can be a challenge.

The Microsoft Partner Network is driven by two forces:

- The need to help partners and customers succeed
- The culture and needs of Microsoft

Therefore to maximise your use of the many benefits available within the Microsoft Partner network it is critical that you understand both your own needs and how Microsoft thinks.

The next few chapters are designed to take you on a journey through these areas and provide you with a structure to reflect. Reflect on your current position, reflect on your strengths and weaknesses and reflect on your opportunity.

Chapter 5: Questions for my organisation

- **Section A** – What do I know about my current and past business performance?
- **Section B** – What is my strategy to maximise my opportunity?
- **Section C** – Do I know and how can I articulate my value proposition?

Chapter 6: Understanding Microsoft

- **Section A** – Tell me about the Microsoft business model, business rhythms and annual performance measurement criteria?
- **Section B** – How should I best represent myself to Microsoft?

Chapter 7: Getting the most from the Microsoft Partner Network

- **Section A** – Business Planning
- **Section B** – Sales and Marketing
- **Section C** – Growing your Skills
- **Section D** – Getting some support

Chapter

Questions for my organisation

When it is obvious that the goals cannot be reached, don't adjust the goals, adjust the action steps

Confucius (Teacher, philosopher and political theorist, 551 – 479 BC)

IN order to make decisions that will enable your organisation to achieve its goals as a Microsoft partner you must begin by being crystal clear on 3 things. First, who are your most profitable customers and what are you delivering to them? Second what is your addressable market opportunity? Third what does success look like, what is your business ambition? In this

chapter we are going to pose some questions and ideas on how you can analyse your business performance, capabilities and metrics and how you can apply the knowledge gained to structure your business growth and remove some of the risks associated with achieving your ambitions.

You need to be making informed decisions about how and where you invest your time and energy to get to where you want to be. You need to be realistic about your priorities and your opportunities.

Most partners acknowledge that a big part of business success is working more strategically with Microsoft and will often say "I want a better relationship". But before you ask for something you need to know what it is you want and what you are prepared to give to get it. If your business message is not clear to you, how can you expect to be able to articulate it to others – and that includes your customers, your partners and Microsoft.

5.1 What do I know about my current and past business performance?

Before you go banging on prospects doors, demanding to see someone, who are you going to say is calling, and why are you there? Do you even know whose door you should be knocking on in the first place?

This first section of questions relate to analysing your business performance. By looking backwards you can clarify how you move forwards. You can bring your failures and successes clearly into focus and begin to understand who you are as a business and what it is you can deliver to your best customers – whoever they may be...?

Once you know yourselves better, you can begin to build your marketing messages, structure your sales function to deliver those to achieve maximum profitability and utilise the tools and resources provided to you by the Microsoft Partner Network. Getting this right will help you to get there faster!

[X]	Question	Why this matters
☐	5.1.1 What has been your business turnover and profitability for the last three years?	Going back any further than three years, means you are analysing information that is no longer relevant in the current climate. Going back only one year, is not going to show you the trends of growth and decline you need to know about to accurately forecast the next few years. With average sales cycles of six to nine months, Looking only at the last twelve months information is simply not enough.
☐	5.1.2 What is your current budget and forecast?	Where are you right now and where are you expecting to be at the end of this financial year? Looking at your current position could highlight some changes you could make NOW that will impact your year-end.
☐	5.1.3 How many people are there in your business?	Classically, a Microsoft partner selling services (people) will generate around £100k of turnover per employee. Obviously that will fluctuate if your business sells a lot of hardware or licenses, as the volume of turnover to margin is vastly different to a people based business. But, as a rule of thumb this is a good place to start understanding if you are over or under staffed.
☐	5.1.4 What do the people in your business actually do?	How many managers, sales people, marketing people, technical people and back office people do you have in your organisation? If you have a dark suspicion that you are carrying too much weight in admin or are putting too much pressure on your best technical consultants, you are probably right. People that have been with the business for a long time but are no longer aligned to the core business growth strategy are only holding you back. If you know that, acknowledge it, and take action, before it has a serious impact.

☒	Question	Why this matters
☐	5.1.5 What are your core capabilities?	What products do you have depth knowledge in? What services are you delivering? You may find that you have an abundance of expertise in an area that you are not exploiting, or indeed are selling things that are outside of your core capability and are therefore difficult and costly for you to deliver.
☐	5.1.6 Where are your target markets?	What you need to identify in a target market, is the definition of the client that you make the most profit from. You may think that your target market is Financial Services and yet you can see from looking through your past sales performance that you actually generate a higher profit margin from organisations within the Public Sector.
☐	5.1.7 What is the definition of the size of organisation you are aiming for?	There is little point in aligning your sales and marketing efforts to attract companies to you that you cannot properly service, at a good profit. You risk ending up with winning a big client, and then tarnishing your reputation by not being able to deliver your promise. Working with other Microsoft partners may be a way to successfully deliver on larger work opportunities. Being realistic about the size of organisations you want to work with is a critical element of achieving business success and an important part of your Microsoft relationship.

☒	Question	Why this matters
☐	5.1.8 Is there an industry vertical you should be focusing on?	You may think that you should scatter your websites and sales collateral with information about every market possible, so as not to miss any opportunities. However the clearer you are about your areas of expertise, the more chance you have to become recognised as market leaders in one particular area. Once you have achieved that you can consider diversification into other markets. For example, if you have clients such as Heinz and Cadbury's, other food manufacturers would be keen to hear about what you have delivered. Ford Motor Company however, as car manufacturers, may be less interested until you have gained recognition as market leaders and can demonstrate your knowledge of "Manufacturing" as a whole. Think of verticals as a "honeycomb", it will help you to decide where one area of expertise can lead into another. There is often a natural attach from one vertical to another. Microsoft is also vertically aligned and offer clear vertical marketing messages. You can only make the best use of these if you know where your target markets are.
☐	5.1.9 What burning issues within the prospect customers business can you resolve?	Have you identified exactly what it is you are able to resolve for your customers business? Market drivers are external forces, business drivers are internal and both are as important as each other. If you are going to present a solution to a prospect customer that will make it part with a reasonable portion of its budget you must be able to communicate your value and demonstrate you know their internal challenges.

☒	Question	Why this matters
☐	5.1.10 Are there key market drivers that you can deliver against?	Burning issues within individual markets are great reasons to invest in technology solutions. For example the smoking ban that was introduced in 2007 caused the hospitality sector significant pain. This forced organisations to invest in new ways of attracting customers. One of those was building new, interactive websites. Another was an investment in improving supply chain processes, leading to high levels of interest in efficient ERP solutions. For Microsoft partners delivering solutions based on the Dynamics platform, this was a fantastic market opportunity.
☐	5.1.11 Who is your target buyer?	Do you know, from analysing deals won over the last twelve months, who it was that actually paid for the solution you sold? What is the job title of the person that holds the budget and what do they care about? It is likely that talking about technology is the last thing your target decision maker wants to hear (and yet all too often as technology experts, partners forget this). What they care about and what they will respond to is how you can demonstrate your understanding of their individual business pains and how you can help them to achieve their individual objectives.
☐	5.1.12 Who are the people that will influence the buying decision?	In addition to your buyer, there are a number of key influencers within the business that are affected by the decision to buy. Do you know who those people are and can you demonstrate your understanding of what matters to them. The more influencers you can reach with your messages the more likely you are to win the deal, as everyone within your prospect agrees that they are making the right choice of supplier.

☒	Question	Why this matters
☐	5.1.13 What is your average deal size?	If you look back over your sales figures what is the most common number that comes up? If your past business performance tells you that you regularly sell £20k solutions, why are you building your sales and marketing plans around chasing deals that are far higher (or lower) than that? Does this sales analysis show that you are getting continual purchase orders that add up to a high value solution for your clients? If that is the case, you could potentially be spending unnecessary pre-sales time and resource that could have been avoided, if you had pitched a higher value sale right at the start to a more strategic decision maker.
☐	5.1.14 How many of your most lucrative clients do you actually have?	The sales people within your organisation hold a wealth of information about individual clients that is rarely tapped into. They will be able to tell you who the best clients are, and the ones that are the most difficult. What you are looking for is depth information about where your income is regularly coming from. How much maintenance time are you investing in individual clients? The hidden costs associated with your sales people spending unnecessary time and effort repairing damage to customer relationships when you have been unable to deliver on time, costs you dear. The more time you have to spend repairing relationships, the less time you have to sell. Knowing the details about how individual clients are managed will help you to make decisions about which clients and therefore markets you should be focusing your efforts on.

☒	Question	Why this matters
☐	5.1.15 Who are your biggest competitors within your target market?	Looking back at deals lost is just as important as looking back at deals won. This is highly valuable information that is often under-estimated within a Microsoft partners business. Going back to clients who didn't give you the business, three or six months later and asking them some intelligent questions about who they selected and why will tell you a lot about your sales process. The lost prospects views of your pre-sales processes, proposals, costs and the solutions you put forward will tell you what you can avoid next time. More than that you may actually find that the deal is not going well and they are glad you called.
☐	5.1.16 What else did the customer buy?	IT purchases are rarely singular. Some well thought through questions to your lost prospect, won customer and/or the people from your company that delivered the solution will tell you what else was or is on the agenda. This could allow you to build out a fuller offering in future proposals.
☐	5.1.17 Looking over past deals are you consistently hiring in extra resources in an area outside of your core capability?	It may be an opportunity to build additional capability within your business. Or if you are coming across the same partners again and again, providing complementary solutions, it may be better to look at formulating more formal partnerships. Partners who partner well with each other are very attractive to Microsoft as more products move off the shelves and supplying more services for the customer makes you a more attractive supplier too. So win-win-win really …

☒	Question	Why this matters
☐	5.1.18 How much of your business is centred on the Microsoft platform?	A Microsoft partner that is looking to improve their relationship with Microsoft, and is asking for opportunities to be passed out, needs to demonstrate that they are committed to Microsoft's technology. It is unlikely Microsoft will engage with you if ninety percent of your business is focussed on competitive technology, or if you haven't even deployed the latest technology in your own office (especially as you get free licences as a partner!). If you can demonstrate that you can provide access to a competitive area of the market, and you are prepared to position the Microsoft platform within that market, you will become very attractive to Microsoft (for obvious reasons). Partners that expect Microsoft to play ball, and yet can only show that a few percent of their overall business is based on Microsoft and have no plans to change, will undoubtedly struggle to get traction.
☐	5.1.19 What versions of software are your customers using?	How much do you know about what upgrade opportunities exist within your existing customers and are you making the most of that? Partners that are driving adoption of new software are very attractive to Microsoft and will quickly be noticed as influential when a new relevant product or solution gets released. The benefits in achieving this reputation are quite substantial and can sometimes generate additional support from Microsoft either from a product manager or marketing lead that is responsible for a developing a specific area of the market.

☒	Question	Why this matters
☐	5.1.20 What is unique about you?	Why you? Why your solution? We have mentioned the importance of looking at the deals you lost – but are you maximizing the information and opportunity from the deals you won? Do you actually know why you were selected (apart from price, which is usually a big consideration for most customers)? The things that a new customer can highlight to you are your strengths and should be driven home to new prospects as much as possible. There is more information about efficient use of customer evidence in the next section.
☐	5.1.21 Is your geographic location relevant to your customers?	Microsoft has recently recognised that there is a need for partners to be supported in local regions, hence the decision to align partner managers and Partner Network experts to local territories. It is far easier (and cheaper) to become a big star in your area, and then grow out, than attempting to be a National supplier. Especially when servicing clients hundreds of miles away can significantly impact your profit margins. If you haven't engaged with your local Microsoft team, you're missing a trick. You can also create a company profile to display in the customer search tool, Pinpoint, which can be created for your specific region so local customers can find you. See the Sales and Marketing section for further details on this.

☒	Question	Why this matters
☐	5.1.22 What is the profile of your ideal customer?	Putting together everything you know about: • Your most lucrative deals • Where you have unique IP, experience or market knowledge • Where you have identified a burning market driver and business driver that you can resolve for potential customers will enable you to create the profile of your ideal customer. Once you have this you can begin to look at your organisation with fresh eyes and plan your strategy to attract and deliver solutions to your ideal customers.
☐	5.1.23 Are you demonstrating how you can help Microsoft to increase market share in a particular solution area or vertical?	If you can demonstrate a clear competitive edge to help increase market share for Microsoft, this will be extremely important over the coming years. As Microsoft gets bigger and broader, so does the competition and they need their partners to be laser focused to help knock out the competition.
☐	5.1.24 Do you have solutions in the market that could deliver business value to a new market?	If you have demonstrable experience and hard ROI metrics available to share with Microsoft about success you have achieved and can research and identify where this could be exploited in another vertical, they would be very keen to hear about that. You need to do your research first though – don't just turn up with an idea that you haven't proven will work and expect Microsoft to put it as a priority. Get the proof first and then have the conversation.

5.2 What is my strategy to maximise my opportunity?

You have looked at your past business performance and understand more about what you are doing that is generating the most profit.

So now that you have looked back, you can begin to look forward, but there is still some analysis to do. The information you have gained about what you are delivering to your customers has undoubtedly raised some more questions that relate to how you can grow and develop your business within your defined target markets.

What you need to consider now, is your addressable market and how you can make the best decisions about where to apply your focus and investment in sales and marketing to attract your best customers (those that match our ideal customer profile).

The questions in this chapter follow a straightforward direction which will enable you to apply your learning, think about your options and ask ourselves how equipped you are to achieve the realistic goals you need to set yourselves?

In this chapter it is still mainly about you. Microsoft's deeper involvement in supporting your success comes later.

☒	Question	Why this matters
☐	5.2.1 Have you defined your business ambition?	Do you actually know what it is you are striving to achieve? Or are you merely working hard every day just to pay the bills and keep the lights on? Setting goals, based on factual analysis of past business success and performance and then setting milestones to achieve those goals, means you are forcing yourself to consistently evaluate your position. It is critical that the ambition and timescales you set yourself are realistic. No-one likes to fail. Setting unrealistic goals such as "being the largest global SharePoint partner in three years", when you are currently a twenty person organisation with a twenty percent focus on SharePoint is probably not helpful.
☐	5.2.2 Have you written a business plan that is aligned to realistic goals?	If you have, do you review it every 6 months? Many niche Microsoft partners see business planning as something they know they should be doing, but really don't have the time for. A business plan does not have to be a three hundred page highly scientific document, which takes months to write, and is therefore not referred to or amended on a regular basis. In order to achieve your business goals, it is far easier to create a simple plan that you consistently develop and mature. It should be one of your most valuable business growth tools as it means you are always making informed decisions.
☐	5.2.3 How many new customers do you need to hit your targets?	Being clear about your new business acquisition targets enables you to consider your marketing efforts. What is your conversion ratio? How many "leads" do you need to win one new project? Having this information begins to help you formulate your marketing strategy.

☒	Question	Why this matters
☐	5.2.4 What are your best routes to market?	This is a huge question and one you need to explore in detail. Firstly, are you 100% focused on a direct sales model, or could you win the increased volume of new business you are looking for through third parties? Lots of partners partner with each other, but this is usually reactive rather than proactive. Others have huge lists of "partners" but find that only a small number actually deliver a return. Often even those that could have a big impact on new business revenues get little attention paid to them. In addition new products or services require serious consideration, as do the implications for hiring new staff to support those decisions. You may consider direct sales as the most effective way to grow your business, but if you are technically minded – how are you going to direct, target and manage your sales function? Lots of partners that are technically led end up with a consistent stream of challenges surrounding the sales function of their businesses. If a direct model is the one for you, bear in mind that you need a professional sales manager to drive that for you. Do make sure you take references and don't end up get "sold to" yourself during the interview process. Only to find that the person you thought was going to transform your business ends up destroying it.

☒	Question	Why this matters
☐	5.2.5 When did you last do a PESTET and/or SWOT?	Successful partners are ones that compete in the current climate not a year ago. Included in your business plan should be an analysis of the current environment from a political, economic, social, technological, ethical and legal perspective (PESTET) – very textbook, yes, but it does actually have a lot of merit if used to identify trends in the market place. Do this first then do your SWOT. Most partners are very self-critical and can give lists as long as their arms of their threats and weaknesses and struggle to define their strengths and opportunities (SWOT). Just because you recognise your weaknesses and threats, doesn't mean you can just leave it there. They are things that need to be addressed. Once you have got into the habit of looking at your SWOT every six months you can prioritise where you should concentrate your actions. There is nothing more satisfying than crossing off negative points because you have taken action to resolve them and they are now strengths and opportunities. Also, taking action to make the most of your opportunities and communicating your strengths through your marketing and business development is even more rewarding.

☒	Question	Why this matters
☐	5.2.6 What is your marketing budget?	What should it be? What is reasonable? This is a difficult question to answer but the most successful partners allocate around three to five percent of turnover (revenue) for marketing. That budget can then be divided between staff and spend – one third for staff, two thirds for marketing spend. Aggressive marketing growth may require more in the short-medium term, but to under-market your business leaves you open to attack from your competitors. You can be sure that they are likely to be investing in creating the biggest noise in the marketplace that they are keen to win the lion's share of.
☐	5.2.7 Do you have the right people in place?	We mentioned in Section 5.1.4 the importance of considering whether you have the right skills in your business, but how does that relate to generating the volume of revenue you need? It could be that unless you were able to charge several thousand pounds per day for your resources (unlikely in the current climate), you simply do not have enough chargeable people available. In addition to thinking about your conversion process, do you have enough sales and marketing people and therefore sales and marketing activity going on to generate the right volume of leads that will achieve the new business targets you have set yourself?

☒	Question	Why this matters
☐	5.2.8　Is everyone in the right roles?	There is a significant difference between new business sales people and account managers. Good new business sales people are just that. They are driven by the new deal and the praise and satisfaction that go along with that. Good new business sales people perform high levels of activity that open up new relationships, often requiring high levels of technical support at pre-sales. They will walk on hot coals for prospects until the deal is won, but may not be the best people to manage a relationship on an on-going basis. Account Managers are very different. A good Account Manager knows his or her customer inside out and is best placed to identify additional opportunities. Have you got your sales people in the right positions? Are you playing to their strengths or forcing them to perform two different functions when they are far better at one, than the other?
☐	5.2.9　What is your recruitment plan?	Do you have one? As you achieve your milestone goals, and your business is growing you need the additional people in place to continue to grow. You also need to consider the ramp-up time required before they are productive and the impact that will have on your revenue figures. Agency fees are of course a big investment but often a far better route to recruitment than the time it takes for you to trawl job sites and deliver countless interviews. Worth considering?

☒	Question	Why this matters
☐	5.2.10 What is your training budget?	There are many different options that are available to you through Microsoft's Readiness team, a lot of which are free. However, some of the highly technical courses are not free and will require investment. Microsoft partners that invest in helping their staff to stay up to date with their technology tend to have a lower staff turnover. Given the speed at which Microsoft releases software, up-to-date training is absolutely critical. In addition to technical training, it is well worth investing in presentation skills training, sales training and marketing training. Just because you have superb technical people, doesn't mean they can present. Most customers "buy in" to technical people as much as sales people during pre-sales. It is well worth developing sharp and professional skills in this area. But don't underestimate the hidden costs. In order for you to measure how effective the training has been and what your actual return has been, you do need to take into account the loss of income that results from sending your people on training courses and ensure you are recouping the full investment you have made. How much of their new skills are people applying? What difference is it making to your bottom line? It's worth knowing that Microsoft has also recently developed a range of "business focused" training courses relevant to partners – using some skilled third parties who specialise in delivering this content. Check out the range of course available in the Partner Learning Centre to stay up to date.

☒	Question	Why this matters
☐	5.2.11 What is the volume of repeat business versus new business?	The importance of good account managers was mentioned previously and how their skills sets vary greatly from your classic new business sales person. The opportunity for up-sell and cross-sell is often missed by partners. Have you given your account manager a set of key information your business needs to know about your customers in order to maximise the sales opportunity? Are they walking away leaving money on the table? If account management is done well then your core set of loyal customers will come back again and again. This can lead to an "80/20 rule" where eighty percent of your business, comes from twenty percent of your customers. Remember the value of these clients to your business and do not take them for granted. Proactively offering discounts to good customers is a great way to keep the competition out and the customer in.
☐	5.2.12 Do you have technical consultants on-site that could be encouraged to generate additional revenues?	We know that a good project can last for a long time, even a smaller opportunity is on average a three month engagement. This often means that technical resources are on site for prolonged periods of time, getting really close to the people that work there. Do you encourage those resources and consultants to develop the opportunity? Do you reward them for it? Another consideration for training is sending some of your technical people on "sales for non-sales people" training courses. The more you can help them to drive additional revenues, the longer the customer relationship will last and the greater the revenues.

☒	Question	Why this matters
☐	5.2.13 Do you have regular sales meetings?	Most partners are technically led; after all it is technology we are selling. But, one thing that needs to be in place is a formalised sales measurement process which enables you to evaluate when to apply time and effort to deals that are in the pipeline. Having a sales meeting whereby each sales person has to justify their existence is one tactic – however, could you consider making the sales meeting a format for open discussion and support and a chance for the right pre-sales investment decisions to be made. You will be amazed at what a productive weekly sales meeting can achieve. Starting off with good news is always best – and make sure you give recognition where it is deserved. Sales meetings should be mandatory – every week, without fail, no excuses.
☐	5.2.14 How much marketing do you do to your existing customers?	Partners are often guilty of consistently looking for new business and new ways to communicate their skills and expertise to new markets. Many partners do not regularly let their existing customers know about new products, services or advice they can offer. Having a regular customer event or monthly newsletter is a great way to build awareness of your brand and keep existing customers up to date (leading to the up-sell and cross-sell). Microsoft provides event and marketing communication vehicles that can support you in this.

☒	Question	Why this matters
☐	5.2.15 How are you ensuring that you are keeping up to date with new products or solutions you could be selling?	Making sure all of the relevant people in your business take responsibility for the things that are going to be relevant to them will enable them build high levels of expertise in their roles – which will pay dividends. Giving one person overall responsibility for being the "catch all" for new information will undoubtedly lead to them staying aware of things that affect them and not the whole business. Microsoft segments information by job role so it's not that difficult for your marketing people to know the strategy and marketing tools available, your sales people know the key sales messages and sales tools and your technical people can talk about and deploy the technology. Microsoft puts the information out there – but how much of it do you actually pick up and utilise?
☐	5.2.16 How are you measuring your customer satisfaction?	Happy customers equal loyal customers. Do you have a clear understanding of what drives your customers, how they feel about you, and whether they intent to purchase from you again? Invest time in understanding your customer base – whether by having conversations directly with your customers, or using a survey tool. Microsoft offers Certified and Gold partners free use of a customer satisfaction survey tool to help with this – see the Sales and Marketing section for more details.

5.3 Do I know, and how can I articulate, my value proposition?

What is a compelling value proposition? What are the different elements that make up the whole? Once you know what your value proposition is how are you going to communicate it?

Microsoft partners are often technically-led and typically seek to differentiate themselves by "just being better" at a certain solution or in a particular technology area. The partners that focus their messaging and develop strong sales and marketing capability enable themselves to stand out from the crowd. You can have the best technology solution or skills on the planet but if you can't market it well and therefore sell it, it's not going to be successful.

Marketing is a highly under-rated skill. Often known as "the colouring-in department", marketing teams spend time and money creating marketing materials and content that is never used. A recent study indicated that sales people, on average use less than forty percent of the marketing materials provided to them. If true this means that sixty percent of your marketing budget may as well be flushed down the toilet. It also means that your sales and technical people are spending their time creating their own marketing materials, presentations and proposals that do not necessarily align to the overall company message or strategy.

Marketing should be a key part of leading the organisation and not follow it. Marketing defines a) who you are as a business and b) who you are selling to – and if done well, conveys that clarity through its messages and materials. Your value proposition is a mixture of both of these things, plus the end customers' value statements. Statements, facts, and ROI figures that enable a prospect customer to realise the high value you can bring to its business and why they should select you as a supplier.

Although some of this information has been referenced in earlier sections, in this section we are going to lay-out the elements of a compelling value proposition and then ask some questions about how you can decide the best way to communicate it.

Remember that if you cannot articulate your value proposition, how do you expect Microsoft to give you the attention you desire?

☒	Question	Why this matters
☐	5.3.1 What is the definition of your target stakeholder organisation?	What is the vertical market? What is the industry? What is the size of organisation? Is it commercial or public sector? Where are they? Companies will respond to information that they can identify with; so being clear on the type of organisation you want to attract and reflecting your understanding of them in your marketing messages will considerably enhance your response rates.
☐	5.3.2 What is the job title of the buyer?	Who is it? Who will buy it and who else will be involved in the decision to purchase? Budgets in businesses sit with individuals. Your value proposition needs to be aligned to the person that actually signs the cheque and the people who will be affected by or influence the decision.
☐	5.3.3 What are the key market drivers?	We referenced market drivers in Section 5.1.10
☐	5.3.4 What are the business pains that can be addressed?	IT budgets are allocated to resolve business issues – prioritised against the things that cause the most pain. The more you can understand about the problems you are solving, communicated as "problem solving" and not technology speak, the more your message will resonate with the customer?
☐	5.3.5 What are your strategic deliverables?	Examples of strategic deliverables are "increased customer retention", "higher average order value" or "increased market share" – strategic wins are the headlines that show you will deliver results and understand what needs to happen as a result of the investment in your products or services.

☒	Question	Why this matters
☐	5.3.6 What are your tactical deliverables?	Tactics are the things you are delivering to achieve the strategy. Using the examples above tactical deliverables to achieve "increased customer retention" could be a new database solution to deliver accurate customer information, a better ecommerce web site which encourages people to buy more leading to "increased average order value" etc …
☐	5.3.7 What are the tangible benefits?	Examples of tangible benefits are statements about saving cash, saving time, reducing costs or increasing revenues. Hard statements that reflect why someone would invest will get a buyers attention.
☐	5.3.8 What are the intangible benefits?	Improved working conditions, lower staff turnaround, addressing green issues, things that add value but cannot necessarily be measured in cash or time. It's not all about cash, sometimes there are other reasons that influence a decision to buy.
☐	5.3.9 What specific customer evidence is available?	The evidence must be relevant to the target market and the stakeholder you are targeting. Microsoft provides partners with access to the vast amounts of customer evidence. You can use this in your marketing campaigns. Obviously, this is much better if the evidence you produce is based on your own customer experiences, but this can be boosted through quoting statements that are in the public domain through the Microsoft partner portal. Many partners talk about being "horizontal" (and we don't mean lying down), but marketing messaging is proven to be far more successful if it is relevant to the target audience.

☒	Question	Why this matters
☐	5.3.10 What is it that you want the prospect to do?	Your value proposition, made up of all the elements quoted above must always be driving prospects towards a specific course of action that you want them to take. That action clearly needs to be an engagement with you in some way, but they need one action, not multiple actions, or they will become confused and do nothing!
☐	5.3.11 What does a really good value proposition look like?	A really good value proposition, your "picture of perfection" will : a) Instantly resonate with your ideal buyer (business and individual) b) Include proof of experience that they can identify with as solving a problem or business pain that they have (business and individual) c) Prompt them into an action which enables you to get closer and start on the cycle of sales with them If your value propositions are not initiating the right levels of interest and generating new business for you – then they need some work!
☐	5.3.12 How can I develop my value proposition to get to market early?	Keep it bang up to date! Make it new, make it fresh and make it clear that you know things your competitors don't! Communicate key snippets of information that you find out about and enhance your messaging to include them. Get your staff subscribing to the right RSS feeds and newsletters and make sure they are taking full advantage of training opportunities – first wave, not second. This may seem risky, but it isn't if you keep focused on your core specialist area and then logically enhance it.

☒	Question	Why this matters
☐	5.3.13 How are you going to reach your ideal buyer?	Trying to attract a CEO within your target organisation to a technical presentation or event is unlikely to succeed. Equally, attempting to communicate with an IT Director via a generic email campaign is unlikely to work. Think carefully about the mechanisms you could use to reach your target audience and which of those are likely to be successful. Microsoft offer different marketing mechanisms through the Partner Network that you can use to support your efforts.
☐	5.3.14 How up to date is your website?	Out of date websites are one of the biggest turn offs for prospective customers. Think about it. You go to all the effort to think through and communicate a targeted value proposition. You develop and invest in high value marketing collateral. This attracts interest from a prospect that goes to your website, only to find none of the information they are looking for. "I know it needs doing but I don't have the time" is a poor excuse for having an out of date website. Most Microsoft partners use the website as one of the only sales and marketing tools they have. It's not working if it is out of date or confusing to the prospect. If your website brings to mind "cobblers children" then you need to do something about that.
☒	5.3.15 How are you measuring your web traffic and your results?	If your website is your only source of marketing collateral then how are you following up on the opportunities it creates for your business? Where do the enquiries go? Who checks that "enquiries at" email address and how often?

☒	Question	Why this matters
☐	5.3.16 Have you thought about the words you are using and do they align to your "ideal buyers" language?	Or are you just talking in technology speak? Lots of partners invest heavily in search engine optimisation (SEO) and then select completely the wrong words. Most business buyers will search for suppliers using business language, they won't necessarily know what the technology is called that will provide the business solution. Worth thinking about?
☐	5.3.17 What is your elevator pitch?	Your elevator pitch must be clear in every form of communication you use about your company. It should be clear everywhere, over the phone, in an email, on your website. Your target prospect must understand what you do in the minimum amount of time. Now that you have thought through your value proposition, go and look at your existing website and marketing material and ask yourself if your target prospect gets it immediately – if they don't, it needs some work.
☐	5.3.18 Do you have a marketing strategy?	Mapping your requirement for the right volume of leads onto a marketing plan starts with a strategy. If your business growth strategy is to become "the largest Virtualisation partner in the South West" what is the marketing strategy you are going to develop to achieve that? A marketing strategy should include elements of customer attrition rate, mapped on to utilisation availability, product development, pricing, relationship management and all elements of the company's overall capability.

☒	Question	Why this matters
☐	5.3.19 Do you have a marketing plan?	A marketing plan is a set of budgeted and measurable activities that will deliver against the marketing strategy. The plan should include how you are going to communicate all the various elements of the value proposition with planned timescales aligned to the business growth ambitions. Marketing planning is another area Microsoft can support partners to develop, but they cannot develop it for you.
☐	5.3.20 How should I carve up my marketing budget and marketing plan between new and existing marketing?	Most (around two thirds) of your marketing budget should be aligned to new business lead generation using your core value propositions. However, do not forget your existing customer marketing or your opportunity to attack competitive technology areas. Segmenting your budget into these three areas and building activities that align to winning new business using opportunities for upgrades, extending your market share, being seen as early adopters or influencing and supporting competitive win strategies will all help to not only grow your business but raise your profile with Microsoft.

☒	Question	Why this matters
☐	5.3.21 Are your sales and marketing teams aligned?	Sales and marketing teams that pull in two different directions can build conflict and dissatisfaction within your organisation and confusion with your customers. The two areas should work together. Marketing defines the strategy and executes against the plan, generating market awareness and subsequently sales leads for the sales teams to pursue. It may sound really simple put like that, but many Microsoft partners do not agree common objectives within these two critical functions. Having a single head of Sales and Marketing can help to pull the two areas together. However the skills required in these areas are different and sometimes two heads may be better than one.

Chapter

Understanding Microsoft

Understanding is a two way street

Eleanor Roosevelt (First Lady of the United States 1884-1962)

PARTNERSHIP. What does that mean to your business and what does it mean to Microsoft? What is it that you can do to understand and then make best use of the resources that the Partner Network provides you with. How do you make the right decisions about where to apply your time and effort to ensure you are making the most of being a Microsoft partner?

In Chapter 5 we discussed the critical importance and value of focusing your business decisions by clarifying your own ambitions, strengths, weaknesses and market opportunities. In this Chapter we are going to explain some of the key motivations and drivers of the Microsoft business, how it operates and what makes it work.

Microsoft is not a marketing or sales organisation, although it invests some $13 billion per year in sales and marketing, a large proportion of which goes into supporting the Microsoft partner community and developing tools and resources that will help partners accelerate growth.

The mistake many partners make is expecting Microsoft to run its business for them. Let's be realistic, if it was going to do that then why would it need to sell through a third party channel?

The Microsoft business has its P&L departments split into key areas, with separate countries run as individual businesses with their own budgets, Managing Directors and Executive boards. In all there are 108 separate subsidiaries, known as "subs", which are basically the individual country offices that make up the Microsoft global business.

The HQ for Microsoft globally is in Seattle and the UK HQ is in Thames Valley Park, Reading with further offices in London, Manchester and Edinburgh. The UK organisation is headed up by Gordon Frazer and is split into two partner groups: Small and Midsized Solutions and Partners (SMSP) and Enterprise Partner Group (EPG). SMSP is led by Scott Dodds and this is the group most of you would interact with, EPG is led by Simon Negus and is primarily for partners working with enterprise customers.

The original mission statement of "a computer on every desk in every home" has now become "the worldwide leader in software and services that help people and businesses realise their full potential"…

Is that current mission statement just "corporate marketing spin" or can you, as a Microsoft business partner ride on the bow wave of success of the world's largest software company and use the tools they give you to make your own fortune?

6.1 Tell me about the Microsoft business

In order to take maximum advantage of your investment in the Partner Network, it is useful to understand what makes the Microsoft business tick. With such a large and complex organisation it is not always easy to get access to the information you need – that is of course, assuming you know what information it is you are looking for!

In this Section we are going to share some facts about the general structure of the business and departments, and what they are there for, the annual business calendar, some of the key job functions and what people in those roles actually do and how they are measured. Probably most importantly what success looks like to Microsoft.

Let's never forget that Microsoft is in business to make money – so whilst some of the decisions made may seem unproductive to us as partners, there is usually a significant amount of in-depth research, careful analysis of past performance, market trends, forthcoming opportunities and a considerable amount of business planning that has gone into them.

Microsoft also may seem "veiled" at times – let's be straight about that – there are many competitive vendors out there that will of course exploit any information that is revealed. So if something is not released, when you think it should be, it could be that it's not being kept back to make life more difficult for you as partners, but often to protect the future of the organisation itself – and subsequently your own businesses.

So if you are sitting comfortably then let's begin.

☒	Question	Why this matters
☐	6.1.1 When does the Microsoft fiscal year run?	1st July to 30th June. Good practice for you to consider the end of year targets and timescales Microsoft are working to. May and June are always extremely hectic and closing business is the key focus during this time of the year.
☐	6.1.2 How is the year divided up in terms of when decisions are made or reviewed?	There are clear times of the year when other activities take over from the usual execution mode. Microsoft splits its year into quarters based on their financial year (July to June). Q1 (July-Sept) is the big planning time, activity is still happening but the focus is heavily on planning. Q2 (Oct-Dec) and Q3 (Jan-Mar) are execution months as usual – with a big review at the end of Q2, when plans may be adjusted according to the results. Q4 (Apr-Jun) is the busiest time as Microsoft focuses on hitting the annual numbers before the year closes, and then it starts planning again. So if you have good ideas about how you can increase revenues for the coming year, then you should be putting them forward to your account manager during April and May to ensure it's included in their plans for the next financial year – you'll get a lot better traction with your ideas at this time of the year.
☐	6.1.3 How does Microsoft segment its customer base? What's the size of a smaller partner or customer?	Microsoft segments its customer base into four categories: Small business (1-24 PCs); Lower mid-market (25-50 PCs); Core mid-market (50-250 PCs); Enterprise (250+ PCs). Thinking of your target audience or customer segment in this way aligns you with Microsoft. This will help Microsoft understand where you are targeting the market and help you to use the marketing tools and resources appropriate to each customer segment.

☒	Question	Why this matters
☐	6.1.4 Can I get lists of who all the Microsoft managed customers are?	No. Releasing information into the public domain (even to partners) about Microsoft's key customer accounts would be commercially dangerous – as of course other vendors work hard to find out this information, the same as Microsoft does when targeting accounts competitively. However, partners that have access to managed customers should most certainly be letting their Microsoft contacts know about that – as it could be that the business could offer support to help you to retain that account – there's nothing like keeping it in the family ...
☐	6.1.5 How is the UK business measured?	Revenue and deployment targets. Like any business Microsoft sub's (countries) are successful or not successful based on hitting performance numbers and getting the technology out there. Most of what the business does is aligned to these goals and should be kept front of mind for partners who are keen to work more closely with the Microsoft business.
☐	6.1.6 How does the account management structure work?	Microsoft has three levels of account management, and the decision on how you are managed dependent on the revenue opportunity and the commitment you show to Microsoft. The structure works as follows: Partner Account Managers; Telephone Partner Account Managers; Partner Network Experts. Your account manager will normally sit in the SMSP department, only enterprise partners are managed in the EPG department. There are also Solution Channel Development Managers who may be assigned to you in your early states of a relationship with Microsoft.

☒	Question	Why this matters
☐	6.1.7 What's the role of a Partner Account Manager?	A Partner Account Manager (or PAM) is an external account manager, who is appointed to support and develop partners. They are responsible for business planning, recruiting, developing and managing named partner accounts and delivering revenue from their partners. Partners are selected to be PAM managed based on various factors, primarily linked to the revenue opportunity. A PAM would typically manage a small number of partners and are more mobile, able to meet regularly with partners on their site and get to know their partners intimately for mutual gain.
☐	6.1.8 What's the role of a Telephone Partner Account Manager?	A Telephone Partner Account Manager (or TPAM) is similar to a PAM except they are telephone based and manage a larger number of accounts. They are predominately revenue focussed and are there to help partners grow their business, engage on opportunities, understand partners' business and help partners use the most relevant Partner Network benefits.
☐	6.1.9 What's the role of a Partner Network Expert?	A Partner Network Expert (PNE) is similar to a TPAM, but they manage a far larger number of accounts and are regionally focussed. A PNE is focussed on being a point of contact and to support and grow partners by advising on key Partner Network benefits, events and opportunities.
☐	6.1.10 What's the role of a Business Manager?	Business Managers (or BMs) are aligned to manage and develop specific customers. BMs cover customers in the EPG, Public Sector and Upper mid-market space.

☒	Question	Why this matters
☐	6.1.11 What's the role of a Solution Channel Development Manager?	A Solution Channel Development Manager (or SCDM) is employed to develop a specific solution channel, usually recruiting and winning over partners that may be selling competitive technology. An SCDM will not directly manage partners but will be an interface for partners that are "less engaged" in certain areas or in the early stages of a relationship with Microsoft.
☐	6.1.12 How can I get my account managers attention?	Again, this is reasonably straightforward. Account managers carry a responsibility for generating revenue and helping you get the most from your Partner Network membership. Microsoft need accurate and current information from you in order to understand the level of support needed to help you. You could be mistaken in thinking that it is a risk to share your requested pipeline with Microsoft, but if you take the decision not to do that, how can you expect Microsoft to know when they should get involved and what it is you need from the relationship. Sharing pipeline is also a pre-requisite of being TPAM or PAM managed. Additionally, partners that communicate and share information with their account manager are much more likely to get more opportunities passed their way, and quickly responded to when they request support. It's a partnership right?

☒	Question	Why this matters
☐	6.1.13 How can I get a Product Managers attention?	If you think (or indeed know) that you are significantly impacting sales of one particular product, can help a product manager to get more customers on the latest version, or influence deployment which is going to help renewal of a licensing agreement, then that is highly valuable and should be communicated. And that will get a Product Managers attention.
☐	6.1.14 What's the joint business planning process with my account manager?	If Microsoft has identified there is high value working together, they will go through a planning process to determine joint aims and goals. There are two internal documents which your account manager may produce as a result of the planning discussion – a Partner Business Plan (PBP) and a Partner Solution Plan (PSP). In reality, only a small number of partners complete a PBP or PSP, it's important that you also have your own business plan as discussed in earlier chapters. The focus of a Microsoft joint business plan is understanding how Microsoft enhances your offering to the marketplace, how your business enhances Microsoft's and what jointly you both will deliver to customers.

6.2 How should I best represent myself to Microsoft?

We included information in Chapter 5 about how you should be making the best decisions about the success of your own business. There is little value in Microsoft investing and working closely with any partner that does not have a clear ambition or marketing strategy and is not clear on its own value proposition and what it is delivering to its customers. Everyone is then working a bit in the dark.

 The most efficient way you can represent your business and subsequent value to Microsoft is by presenting a clear and consistent message. A message that gives individual Microsoft stakeholders confidence that you understand your customers and markets. A message that shows you can communicate that to prospects. Individuals you work with will also know what's relevant to you and make sure they keep you updated with the right information.

Being clear and current makes you a good bet and a low risk.

Reporting your successes is one of the key ways to get attention. Hard ROI (Return on Investment) metrics are the real winners and combined with customer evidence, this is one of the best ways to attract new clients. The more you are willing to share your metrics and wins with Microsoft, the more valuable you become and the more opportunities you will receive.

In this section we are going to ask the questions to help you ensure you are communicating the right information in the best way, and that you are representing yourself as you want Microsoft to see you. A way that is easy to understand and will instantly resonate with the right people within the Microsoft business.

☒	Question	Why this matters
☐	6.2.1 What is the best way to ensure Microsoft are clear on the value I can bring to the business?	Think through your value proposition to Microsoft and summarise the facts, the experience you have and the value you can add in a one page A4 document. Then make sure your account manager has it and understands it. If you don't have an account manager, you do need to ensure the message on the home page of your website is clear, so that Microsoft (just the same as anyone else) can instantly understand what it is that you do. Additionally, maximise use of the tools made available through the Partner Network for representing your customer evidence, which we will discuss in detail in the next Chapter.
☐	6.2.2 Why shouldn't I just have loads of meetings in the Atrium at Thames Valley Park, surely that way everyone will know who I am and I'll get more traction?	Working at Microsoft is not just a job; it's a way of life. There is a high level of commitment and input required and a considerable quality of output that is expected from Microsoft staff (whoever they may be). Microsoft employees who are driven to support partners and help them to grow their businesses' will always try to help and will therefore usually accept invitations to meet. However, given the performance and results people have to deliver, partners will see much greater value in working with a smaller network of people within the business, whose objectives align to theirs. No-one really has time just for coffee, (well not more than once anyway) unless there is a valid reason for connecting and both parties can realise mutual return. Keeping it relevant is the best way to get the right traction.

☒	Question	Why this matters
☐	6.2.3 Why should I invest in attending the Worldwide Partner Conference?	A multitude of reasons. The Worldwide Partner Conference (WPC) is the place to find out all the latest information on the development and evolution of the Microsoft platform, tools and technologies. Along with the key marketing strategies that Microsoft plan on driving out in the coming year, supported with the resources available in the Partner Network to help you deliver the same message to your customers. WPC is can be looked at as essentially highly subsidised training. Where else can you get access to some of the world's leading authorities in sales, marketing, business and technical speaking direct to you? Then of course there's the networking with Microsoft staff and other partners. Microsoft UK in particular makes a substantial investment in WPC and pulls out all the stops to ensure UK partners are kept well informed, connected and entertained throughout the week. Relationships built at WPC can last a lifetime and will reap rewards time and time again.

☒	Question	Why this matters
☐	6.2.4 Is it important that I attend events as far as raising my profile with Microsoft is concerned?	There is never a substitute for face to face contact. If you are keen to develop a reputation for being fully engaged and on board with the Partner Network, then that is often well demonstrated by your attendance at relevant events (Microsoft and other partners can see that you are serious). However, there are some partners that think it would be in the best interests to attend everything – and that is not the case. As with all areas of the Partner Network, staying focused and concentrating on your own business is key. The more successful you are, the more valuable you become – master of your trade, rather than jack of all is without doubt the best way to show your commitment and specialisation. By attending the events suited to your focus you will gain the value from the product teams, networking, and training, and be more aligned with the Microsoft roadmap. Sometimes although not publicised, announcements and offers are made to attendees of those events that are not made elsewhere.

☒	Question	Why this matters
☐	6.2.5 How important is it to be seen as specialising in a product or industry?	The "hero's" within the Partner Network, specialise and build a reputation for being brilliant at one thing. It's not difficult to see on the partner portal the partners that do that and you can clearly see the results they have achieved from their efforts. Competencies within the Partner Network have been designed to enable specialisation in a big way, and that message is only going to get stronger as the programme matures. The speed at which technology matures forces us all too consistently develop our skills and mature our solutions, so even if you do specialise in one area, you will still be driven to evolve – that's the nature of IT, especially within the world that is Microsoft!
☐	6.2.6 How much and how detailed does customer reference information need to be to generate interest within Microsoft?	You may be concerned that you do not have enough information to create a large case study and therefore don't share your news. However the key is the quality rather than the quantity. Microsoft has experts who can create a story around your basic facts provided that at the heart there is a compelling fact or piece of evidence. Having a case study written by Microsoft holds great value as it means you can direct any potential customers to the Microsoft website containing your case study which is marketing your company's solutions. This proves the commitment and expertise you show to your customers. Creating solutions that have added value to a Microsoft product over a Microsoft competitor will also get you noticed within Microsoft.

☒	Question	Why this matters
☐	6.2.7 Will providing case studies be seen positively?	Case studies are a key piece of sales and marketing collateral for any business. They highlight how real customers are using the vendor offerings. Microsoft is no different. It is worth remembering that Microsoft's marketing is focused on their current or soon to be launched offerings. So think about how your story fits with this and then talk to your account manager. They should be able to find out if there is a current need for case studies in your area and put you in touch with the right people. But don't be surprised if your fantastic customer story highlighting the use a Windows 2000 and SQLServer 6.5 doesn't get an immediate reaction!
☐	6.2.8 How should I structure my business plan, to ensure it resonates well with Microsoft?	The key here is ensuring that your business plan aligns with Microsoft goals for the current fiscal year. The best way to understand this is to watch the keynote sessions from the Worldwide Partner Conference (either in person or online) – this event is held at the start of Microsoft's fiscal year and this is where the corporate executives will outline their priorities, and the UK executives will outline the specific UK goals. Once you have this information, you should review your business plan and align it to match tightly with the Microsoft goals.

☒	Question	Why this matters
☐	6.2.9 What are Microsoft's rhythms and how will understanding these help me?	All business have areas where they focus their investments. In Microsoft speak these are "rhythms" and are aligned to the coming years big investment bets. Understanding what these are will allow you to align your requests for assistance with areas that have resources. The rhythms for 2010 cover areas such as Windows 7, Office 2010, Azure and Online Services.
☐	6.2.10 How often should I be talking with my account manager?	Your account manager is your inroad to Microsoft. This person will hold the torch, and will help you get where you want to go. So it's only common sense that you will succeed better if you have a good relationship with your 'torch bearer'. However, your account manager will manage multiple accounts, and it won't always be possible to have weekly phone calls. So the best plan is to setup a regular rhythm of communications with your account manager, working this out with your account manager based on their availability – which may be monthly, or even quarterly. And get it booked in - once it's in their diary, they'll stick to it. Then make sure you have an agenda set before every call/interaction and share this with your account manager – then follow up with any actions. It's general business practice, but it's surprising how many people don't think to do this with their account manager.

Getting the most from the
Microsoft Partner Network

If it's the Psychic Network why do they need a phone number?

Robin Williams (Comedian and Actor, 1951 –)

WHERE do you start to articulate what it actually means to be a successful Microsoft partner? How about the value of the brand in itself? Any qualified marketing or PR person will tell you building brand value, building brand value and building brand value are the three things that can take a successful business to a highly successful and therefore very valuable business. Microsoft is the third most valuable brand in the world, with an overall brand value of $59,007m as measured by Interbrand, Best Global Brands Study 2008 and rated the third most influential bench mark by CEO's (Coca Cola is the top brand in case you were wondering oh, and Google is still only sitting at Number 10). So, to begin with as a Microsoft partner you have access to co-branded materials with the most valuable software company in the world. That's not a bad starting point wouldn't you say?

However there are additional benefits available through the Microsoft Partner Network and these are both vast and varied. The previous chapters about understanding your goals and ambitions and understanding Microsoft are critical precursors to exploring these benefits. Without these insights it would be all too easy to get lost in the mass of resources.

As with any large programme, things change, are added or removed. Keeping up to date with these updates will ensure that you continue to get the best return on your investments.

 Subscribe to partner RSS feeds so that changes are pushed to you rather than you having to chase them.

http://www.microsoft.com/uk/partner/rss

 In summary you need a clear focus on your needs to effectively navigating the vast resources and benefits available as part of the MPN. The greater your focus and the more you put in, the more you will get out.

http://www.microsoft.com/uk/partner/kickstart

7.1 Business Planning

In this Section we are going to describe how to best utilise the Business Planning tools available through the Microsoft Partner Network many of which are heavily under-utilised by partners. Instead of using the free tools provided as part of the Partner Network, it is highly likely that you are spending valuable budget with third parties, using in-house resources or just not doing it at all. Which does seem rather costly and unnecessary.

The majority of partners, (as we have discussed in earlier chapters) are not created by business, sales or marketing people, rather they are technically expert. The businesses have grown organically with a technical mind-set and have  developed through referral and winning repeat business from existing clients. The majority of partners were not created by business, sales or marketing people – therefore Microsoft makes a considerable effort to produce sales and marketing tools and materials that keep that in mind. There are a range of services available for partners to use, most of which have accompanying guides and FAQ's, so that technical experts do not need to have a marketing degree to use them effectively.

It is worth remembering that Microsoft is providing materials that often need to cover an incredibly diverse range of technologies, solutions, vertical markets and partner size and types. So don't expect each set of templates or materials to exactly match your specific business. If in any area you don't use the whole thing, you can still review the information provided and get some really great ideas about how you can apply the content in your own business.

☒	Question	Why this matters
☐	7.1.1 Should I be engaging my account manager when I'm business planning?	Yes. Effective account management is one of the keys to business success but to do it effectively is not always that straightforward. There are a lot of insights your account manager can provide to help with your planning. There are whitepapers, sales guides and account planning templates available on the partner portal (free for partners) which will help make the discussions with your account manager as valuable as possible.
☐	7.1.2 Does Microsoft provide anything to help me with assessing my business performance?	Yes. Check out the Partner Profitability Assessment tool. This is an online survey available to all partners which takes about twenty minutes to complete and generates a customised report enabling you to benchmark your business against similar Microsoft partners. The report is confidential and you can download the questions and a sample of the report you will get before you start. The report will help you to consider how your business measures up against your competitors and it enables you to benchmark your business performance against industry analysis and trends. This is particularly useful if you are considering expanding or extending your existing services into new areas and may enable you to reduce some of the associated risks. You can use the outcomes of the assessment to make more informed decisions about where you need to invest or focus on specific areas of your business. You can also use the CSAT survey tool to understand how your business is performing with your customers – see the 'driving loyalty' question below for more details on this tool.

☒	Question	Why this matters
☐	7.1.3 Has Microsoft commissioned any reports specific to Microsoft Partner Competencies?	Yes. If you go to the Business Planning Research page on the portal you can find IDC research relevant to specific Competencies. This is refreshed regularly so would be beneficial to check back on a monthly basis to see what is new.
☐	7.1.4 What industry information is available?	All partners can get access to a range of Business Planning Research information which Microsoft has collected from IDC (a global provider of market intelligence and advisory services for the IT, telecommunications and consumer technology markets) and Gartner (a world leader in IT research and advice). Regular research is provided in specific solution areas and can be accessed and downloaded. Some reports cost significant amounts of money (£thousands), so if you are a regular buyer of analyst reports its worth checking the portal first to see what is available before you spend your own hard earned cash.
☐	7.1.5 What about Business tools for my prospects and customers – what's available for me to use?	Check out the Business, Technology and Security Assessment toolkits. These will help you, to help your customers come to logical conclusions about how your solutions can save them money and/or increase profits. These tools take prospects through a step by step process and then enable you to demonstrate tangible benefits either technically or business focused that will aid you when justifying the required investment. The toolkits include a reporting functionality so you can provide your customers and prospects with the results of their assessment.

☒	Question	Why this matters
☐	7.1.6 What are Solution Accelerators? Are they useful for Business Planning and if so how?	Solution Accelerators are a set of automated tools and guides which you can use to help your customers address key concerns like infrastructure management, communications, collaboration, security and regulatory compliance. Solution Accelerators enable you to deploy solutions more quickly as a lot of the functionality is pre-built. This enables you to shorten the pre-sales phase, free up your resources to add more value to customers and extend the size and scope of deals you can bid for and win. They also help to reduce risk by providing guidance and IP on best practice.
☐	7.1.7 I hear a lot about Infrastructure Optimisation, but I don't really get it. What should I be aware of and what is the value to me?	Infrastructure Optimisation (IO) is all about enabling customers to understand more about how they can make optimum use of their investment in IT. The Microsoft model is centred on enabling you to change your customers use and view of IT from "Basic to Dynamic" and will assist you with positioning the difference between IT being merely operational (delivering the basic function) to maximising its overall value to the business so that it delivers reductions in cost and helps to maximise their profitability. The model Microsoft has built breaks down depth analyst and academic research into a simple and logical step by step process. If you can make the time to understand the IO model it may help you to have much bigger conversations with your prospects and customers and extend the size of the opportunities you talk about with them.

☒	Question	Why this matters
☐	7.1.8 What specific tools are available for me to use to communicate the Microsoft IO model?	Firstly there is a downloadable Executive Summary that describes the three focus areas surrounding optimisation of Core Infrastructure Optimisation (Core IO), Business Productivity (BPIO) and Application Platform (APIO) Additionally it describes how the different areas of optimising your IT can deliver real business value, and where the Microsoft products and solutions slot in to the model. There is also a video that describes how the model can help customers to effectively manage their business and gives an example about how partners can get started. Of course this is supported by a range of On Demand Online Webinars, Exams and Online Tutorials covering the full range of products and solutions details. You can find these by searching on the Partner Learning Centre.
☐	7.1.9 How can I find the right people within Microsoft who will help drive my business?	Microsoft individuals that have the same objectives as you can be highly valuable contacts who can provide you with the right information and support your business. If you can identify your key strengths and objectives, your account manager, or key contact, can help identify the right people to help you. But remember that you need to be very clear about what you are looking for – Microsoft is a maze and it's easy to get lost. In addition, Microsoft staff do changes roles from time to time so it is often much more beneficial for you to build a relationship with the business rather than an individual by being clear on your business value and making sure your Microsoft contacts are all aware of it.

☒	Question	Why this matters
☐	7.1.10 What if I've just picked up the 'responsibility' for managing the Microsoft relationship?	Take time to understand where you currently stand with your partnership. Check the partner membership centre (accessed from the partner portal) to get a view on your account status e.g. which Competencies have you achieved. Remember, Competencies are how Microsoft labels you, and you will be treated accordingly – so make sure you're representing yourself as you wish to be seen. You can also use the partner dashboard, again on the portal, to see at a glance how many of your staff are taking training, how your customers are rating your company, how many leads you're generating through the sales tools and more. If you have more red lights than green lights, identify the areas for improvement and include in your plan. If you have an account manager, make sure you do this background research before your first meeting and you'll start off on the right foot.
☐	7.1.11 Why should I share my pipeline with Microsoft?	If you want more leads, you need to have a robust way of reporting on them and you need to be able to demonstrate to Microsoft that you are a partner that they should be passing leads to. Being completely transparent with your pipeline with Microsoft will benefit you.

☒	Question	Why this matters
☐	7.1.12 I want to encourage customer loyalty as much as I can. What does Microsoft provide to help me with this?	The first step is to take time to understand your customers much better. Microsoft offer a service to Certified and Gold partners, run by external market research organisation TNS, which allows you to survey your customers and get powerful information about their opinions of you and their purchasing behaviour. We talked in Chapter 5 about how you need to put some time in to understand more about the value you bring to your customers – well, here's the way Microsoft provide for you to do that. At no cost, you can essentially gain insight into your customers ROI through advanced analytics. Try to lead your customers to answer the questions that are of most value to you, such as purchasing cycles and key performance metrics, increase awareness of your brand. For-warned is for-armed, so if you know how a customer feels about what you are doing (good or bad) you can do something about it. You can also use the positive information for marketing, and the information gained about buying cycles to get the insight you need to sell and extend your customer reach.

☒	Question	Why this matters
☐	7.1.13 I'm planning my marketing activity. Is there anything I get as a partner that will save us money and time with this?	Yes. There are huge amounts of marketing tools and resources that will save you money. Before you start trying to create your own materials, why not first see if what you need is already on the portal. If it's not quite what you want, you can still get some fantastic ideas and content which will get your campaigns out the door far faster. Most of us will never have the same budget that Microsoft has to drive interest in the platform or reach quite the same range of customers and prospects, so save yourself time and effort by piggy-backing on the Microsoft campaigns rather than building your own. Also, download the partner marketing plan for free instead of writing your own from scratch, and then just tailor it to suit your own business.
☐	7.1.14 I need to save money this year, how do I make sure I'm making best use of the free software licences for running my business?	Microsoft provides free licences for most of their products to partners, dependent on your tier level and programme. You can get a clear view of how many licences and which products, by checking the licence statement on the partner membership centre. There are ways to 'earn' more licences – like getting a new Competency, adding more office locations to your account, or moving up a tier level. And remember, all of these licenses can be used to run your business – don't pay for it, when you get it for free!
☐	7.1.15 How will running the software I am licensed for help my sales?	There is no substitute for hands on experience. The more of the software and solutions you are selling that you have embedded in your business, the more likely your sales people are to wax lyrical about the benefits.

☒	Question	Why this matters
☐	7.1.16 How should I navigate the partner portal to find the benefits I need?	The partner portal has been broken into separate tabs which are roughly based on your job role – if you don't know what you're looking for, then you should start by browsing the tab which relates best to you. So if you work in sales and marketing – the best place for you to start is the sales and marketing tab. Equally it you're technical, go to either the product tab or the support tab. If you're managing the Partner Network membership, the programme membership is the tab for you. If you know what you're looking for, then you should use the search function to find the exact page.

7.2 Sales and Marketing

Now that we have explored the range of Business Planning tools, which includes some tools to help with your marketing plan, it seems like the right time to look at the extensive range of sales and marketing resources in more detail.

Once again, clarifying your focus and business direction is key to maximising your use of the resources available. Not only will doing this help you to communicate your value better to customers and

attract more of the right kind of new customers, it will also help you to segment the areas of the portal you use, and how you use it.

Many partners don't take advantage of the tools available to them on the partner portal. Some simply don't know the benefits exist. For others it just seems too much time and effort to invest in understanding where to find the things they are looking for.

Apart from the technical areas of the Partner Network and the portal we would suggest that the sales and marketing tools are the biggest part. And, as with all other areas, have to cover and communicate a vast amount of information - given the Microsoft platform now includes over three hundred products, you can understand why that is.

We don't want this section to be a guide on how to use the partner portal but it is important to mention that until you are familiar with where things are 'filed' the most effective way to use the partner portal, to find the information you are looking for, is to use the search function.

If you can't find something then talk to your account manager or the Microsoft Ask Partner helpline.

There are a series of on-demand videos that provide a walk-through of the portal. These are fantastically valuable for people who are new to the partner portal.

☒	Question	Why this matters
☐	7.2.1 New sales leads are the most valuable things to me. Is there a place where I can promote myself to customers and prospects?	Yes. Microsoft has a customer search engine to allow customers to search for Microsoft partners by solution area and geography – this is called Pinpoint. On this search engine there is also the option for customers to provide feedback and ratings on partners – so an opportunity for you to actively show your value to customers. You've got to be in it, to win it. Take time to create a well written profile, using the profile entry tool, Solution Profiler, and you'll be added to the Pinpoint search results. Make sure you check out your competitors profiles, see what they're writing and make yours better. And search on your postcode – if you're low on the search results, see what you need to do to come top.
☐	7.2.2 What are the key things that will make a difference to my profile on Solution Profiler?	Tailor it to your audience. Make it about your customers and the results you have delivered as much as possible. Use the language appropriate to the type of customer (and/or buyer) you are hoping to attract. Include ROI statements if you have them and keep the description really clear and succinct. Better to do a few short solution profiles that are to the point and capture your prospects attention, than trying to write one big profile that covers everything you do - people will not necessarily read it all. Follow the advice from the question above and check out your competitors profiles. Also, make sure there are no spelling mistakes or grammatical errors – that's just shoddy and does not give the best first impression to potential customers or prospects.

☒	Question	Why this matters
☐	7.2.3 How do I find other partners to work with?	There's a tool provided by the Partner Network called Channel Builder, and this is where Microsoft encourages partners to look for each other. You can use this to find partners that could extend your geographic reach, or are keen to go to market in the same area as you with a complementary solution. There is also the opportunity to strengthen your chances of winning customer deals you may already be working on. Picture the scene. You have a customer opportunity and your competitor has a relationship with another partner that will enable them to extend the size and scope of the solution provided to the customer. You could be out of the running, having spent months getting the opportunity to this stage. You need another partner that is as committed as you are to Microsoft and one that is proven to have the experience you are looking for to stand a chance of winning the deal. Where will you go to find that partner? Bing? Google? How about Channel Builder as a good place to start? There's also the Microsoft Partner Community (online discussion based forum) which you can use for informal networking with other partners.

☒	Question	Why this matters
☐	7.2.4 How can I leverage Microsoft PR?	Did you know that as a partner you get access to PR materials for free? If you email the PR team (*ukppr@microsoft.com*) you can request a pre-written press release, which you can tailor to your company, and you can use this to announce your status in the Partner Network e.g. If you've just earned the Business Intelligence Competency, or you've just reached Gold. This press release will also include a quote from a Microsoft executive to add credibility. If you are just looking for a quote from a Microsoft executive to use in your marketing collateral, you can also request this from the PR team.
☐	7.2.5 How can Microsoft help me to build credibility with my customers?	There are a range of ways. You may want to consider entering yourself for a Microsoft partner award (entries open around April). If you end up as a runner-up, or winner, you'll get recognition from Microsoft which you can use in your own PR or marketing. It sounds simple, but are you using the Microsoft partner logo on your website? Have you thought about getting a quote from a Microsoft exec to use in your press releases? Have you used the Microsoft facilities for holding your own event? Have you deployed the latest software that Microsoft gave you free licences for? Customers and prospects will often ask "do you use it"? If the answer is yes, it can only add to your belief in the value of the product ort solution. Simple things, but all available to you as a partner, and all this adds to your credibility.

☒	Question	Why this matters
☐	7.2.6 I see partners being quoted in Microsoft's marketing, what makes them more special than me?	Nothing – they are simply playing the game better. If you want to get included in Microsoft's marketing, get yourself involved in the new projects the marketing team are piloting, then you'll naturally be on the 'list' of partners they turn to when they need a quote for that project. How do you find out about new projects? Read the partner newsletter – it's the marketing teams primary communications vehicle. Another tip – say something positive. Human nature is such that we only give feedback when it's negative, try giving positive feedback (but be honest!).
☐	7.2.7 I've just reached Gold and/or I've just got a new Competency. What now?	Well, how about telling your customers? You can get pre-written press releases from the partner PR team (*ukppr@microsoft.com*) to announce your new status to your customers – and it includes a quote from a Microsoft executive to add strength to your press release.

☒	Question	Why this matters
☐	7.2.8 How can I increase Microsoft's awareness of my organisation?	Increase your visibility with Microsoft by maximising use of all the tools and resources available to you and all the relevant communication methods you have access to as a partner. As discussed in Chapter 6 that doesn't mean just trying to have coffee with every member of Microsoft staff. But definitely try to get to the Microsoft events that interest you, attending in person will show commitment and is noticed. Also be proactive using the tools and resources in the Partner Network and then feedback on tools/resources. This can sometimes get you on the radar with the Partner Network managers who are often looking for partners to be involved in pilot projects. But remember, these projects will always come with a time investment request, so only get involved if you can really commit. But your involvement will help build your visibility. Also, if you're had any significant wins, especially with Microsoft competitors, then tell Microsoft about this. You might just get used for a case study which is one of the most powerful marketing tools. If you're a partner selling licences, the best form of licenses to sell to get you noticed are from Authorised Microsoft distributors. These distributors report back to Microsoft on a monthly basis telling them what has been sold and who to.

☒	Question	Why this matters
☐	7.2.9 Microsoft seem to run a lot of events, how do I know which ones to attend to get me 'noticed'?	Ok, firstly, events aren't just about getting noticed. Microsoft events are great because they are mainly free, and are an easy way to keep up to speed with launches, changes etc. You'll also get to see who is involved on the Microsoft side in a particular area (useful for follow up questions and building your network), and you can meet partners who are interested in the same area. But make sure the events are relevant to you. Use the RSS feeds on the portal to have events pushed to you. Not all events are as well/openly promoted as others so make sure that your account manager knows that you are interested in events in specific areas.
☐	7.2.10 Can I run my own event at the Microsoft office?	Yes, although this is limited by your level in the Partner Network, the purpose of your event and is subject to availability (some times of the year are busier than others). Gold and Certified partners can run up to four events per year using the Microsoft facilities, which includes Microsoft advertising your event on their website, providing a nice room and an event hostess to make sure your event runs smoothly – all for free. You may also be able to secure a Microsoft speaker for the event if you make the right connections, and have a good value proposition. When you are working so hard to generate demand and get customers and prospects to events, it is critical that all attendees have a good experience and want to work with you, which is what you'll get when you use the Microsoft facilities.

☒	Question	Why this matters
☐	7.2.11 Microsoft technology is always changing. How do I make sure my sales teams are always up to date?	Give each member of your team a copy of the Microsoft Sales Toolkit. This is the bible to Microsoft products. It is updated every six months with all the latest products and holds information to help you sell it, such as the customer conversations you should be having, and the up-sell opportunities to increase your deal size. Additionally, make sure you are deploying all the free licences you get for Microsoft products – this allows your sales staff to become experts on the software before going out to customers.
☐	7.2.12 I spend a lot of time creating materials to help me sell Microsoft products – I'd rather just sell. What do I get as a partner?	If you spend a lot of time creating presentations, use the Microsoft Toolkits. These are a set of rich, interactive presentations which are designed to provide in depth information around a specific topic area for a defined target audience. If you spend your time building out customer specific demos from scratch, use the Demo Showcase instead. Use it to find relevant product demos that show off the technology to the best of its ability, which really helps your customers to see the value and power of the products - at no cost. For general sales information, check out the Partner Sales Resource mini-site. This provides white papers, case studies, demos, templates, presentations, best practice guides and technical information for your solution area and customer type.

☒	Question	Why this matters
☐	7.2.13 What do my sales team need to know about licensing?	It will be easier to sell your services if you are able to leverage the customers' investments in software, so your sales and pre-sales teams should understand the basics of EA (Enterprise Agreements), Select, Hosting, Open Licensing etc. It also helps to make sure that the customer is properly licensed as otherwise they are exposed to running illegal software. Do you undertake an Asset Management review when planning a deployment project? This will help you to get some answers and present and recommend the right solutions.
☐	7.2.14 How can I get my sales teams telling the same story as Microsoft?	By deploying the software internally your sales people will be able to talk from experience about how they use the software and the improvements they have seen happening in their own businesses as a direct result of the investment.
	7.2.15 Why should I get Microsoft to create my case study?	Although you may see the benefit of case studies the physical act of creating one can be daunting. If Microsoft decides they like your story then they instruct a third party company who specialise in this area and it is their responsibility to make it happen. They will talk to you and your customer and ensure that the end product looks professional and is approved by all parties.

☒	Question	Why this matters
☐	7.2.16 How does creating a case study with Microsoft help my sales and marketing?	Case studies are good in the first place as they show your capabilities validated by your customer. By working with Microsoft you add to this the associated with a global brand. Microsoft does not spend money creating case studies for them to be hidden. They use them at events and make them available via the Microsoft Case Studies web site (*http://www.microsoft.com/uk/casestudies/*). All of this provides you with external validation of your skills and may even help to address that awkward objection as you try and close a sale. You also have the rights to reuse the case studies for your own marketing efforts.

7.3 Growing your skills

Keeping up to speed with Microsoft's range of products and the industry trends that are driving the market can be daunting.

Microsoft recognises that in order to sell more, it needs to invest in its sales force – partners! Microsoft has to work hard to keep its sales force up to speed with developments in the products, assist them with how they can profitably go to market and provide access to sales, marketing and technical support during and after the sale has happened.

As a member of the Partner Network you have access to training on the latest software, solutions, products and licensing on-line. The majority of this is provided at no cost or heavily subsidised.

This does not just cover the technical product areas. Microsoft also offers a range of courses, webinars and online tutorials covering sales, marketing and business training. Many of these have been created or are delivered by external third party domain experts. These will not only develop and accelerate the skills of your technical pre-sales people, but will help your sales people to sell more effectively.

There are also the annual gatherings such as the Worldwide Partner Conference and the Professional Developer Conference. These provide high intensity learning opportunities as well as networking with other partners and Microsoft.

Add to this the events that are organised in Microsoft offices and you have a comprehensive set of resources to ensure that you stay up to speed with Microsoft.

☒	Question	Why this matters
☐	7.3.1 Microsoft runs so many events and I don't always have the time to attend everything I get invited to. How can I get access to the information I need without spending days and days out of the office every month?	Most Microsoft events that are delivered face to face (i.e. You going to the HQ office in Reading or the London office) are also available online. In fact, you can actually request online content, if you have registered for an event and then find you are unable to attend. All of the content delivered at WPC (Worldwide Partner Conference – see 6.2.3) is available live online during the session and afterwards through the partner portal. Some sessions are of course best face to face, particularly depth technical sessions where you have the opportunity to ask direct questions of the instructor, or depth sales and marketing sessions where you have the opportunity to process content delivered and can ask questions specific to your business and its challenges.
☐	7.3.2 I'm a techie. What Microsoft events should I attend?	Microsoft plan and execute huge variety of events which will be relevant to your specialisation and area of expertise. Some are local and relatively small whilst others are regional or global. The main events that are attended by thousands of people from the UK are Tech-Ed Europe, Professional Developers Conference (PDC), MIX and Microsoft Management Summit (MMS).

☒	Question	Why this matters
☐	7.3.3 Why are the requirements for certification changing for the Microsoft Partner Network?	In order to stay up to date with the ever changing technologies, certification on the new products shows an understanding and commitment to Microsoft products. It increases the value of partnering and enhances customer satisfaction. The Microsoft Partner Network has itself been founded on the core values of Microsoft with a commitment from Microsoft to get their own staff certified. By increasing the requirements for the Advanced levels it proves expertise within the Competencies.
☐	7.3.4 What training resources are available to train our techies for the new Partner Network requirements?	The Partner Learning Centre gives you access to technical training, much of which is provided free or at discounted rates, so this should be your first port of call. E-learning from Microsoft is a great resource often with free online and downloadable courses to get to understand new and existing products. Also, read the partner newsletter, you may see free or discounted exam vouchers, or Microsoft subsidised on-site courses being advertised. Attending events held throughout the UK optimises your knowledge throughout the Microsoft portfolio, with Tech-Ed being the major technical event held globally with a high concentration of training resources and instructor led courses all included in the entrance fee.

☒	Question	Why this matters
☐	7.3.5 How do we get qualified?	Microsoft exams are sat exclusively at Prometric testing centres that are sited all over the UK. Exam bookings can be made online at *www.prometric.com* or by phoning any Prometric testing site. Prometric exam results are displayed immediately to candidates, and are then uploaded to the Prometric servers with passing candidates results forwarded on to Microsoft for inclusion in their system. You can then align this certification to a Competency, in the partner membership centre, to achieve a new Competency.
☐	7.3.6 Are there any communities which I should be using to connect with other Microsoft techies?	The Online Technical Communities are provided on the partner portal. These are technical communities for partners to communicate with each other (and with Microsoft techies) to learn more about key technologies, share ideas and get answers to specific challenges. The number of communities is vast and there is one relevant to virtually every area of the Microsoft platform. If you have any "genius techies" in your organisation, this is where they can help you even further to elevate your position and get recognised as highly valued professionals within the technical community. Microsoft's own support professionals also monitor the communities carefully and respond to all questions raised there.

☒	Question	Why this matters
☐	7.3.7 Can I get access to Microsoft technical staff to help my teams grow their skills?	There are two options you can choose from. There are a team available over the phone that can run live meeting technical training for your staff – this service is called Technical Advisory Support. It is free for Gold partners and partners who have the ISV Competency, but other partners can purchase support hours. There are also a team of staff who can visit your office to provide technical knowledge, this is called Partner Advantage and you have to purchase a contract to use this service. But remember, there's a vast amount of training online – so review this first.
☐	7.3.8 There are so many training courses, is there an easy way to understand which courses I should take?	There are a series of learning paths which are designed to help you navigate through the training and other resources that are available for Microsoft products and solutions. Simply go to the Microsoft Learning Centre homepage and select the product or solution area, and the type of training (e.g. technical, sales, marketing) and you'll be presented with a list of the core and optional training courses that Microsoft recommend taking.
☐	7.3.9 I don't have the bandwidth to send people on 3 or 5 day training courses, but need to keep up to date, what can I do?	Microsoft has wised up to this and is providing a number of ways to provide marketing, sales, technical and licensing readiness and training. It is providing materials through instructor led classes, workshops, live meetings, recorded live meetings or webcasts, virtual instructor led classes, hands on labs and e-learning; so there is now a training mechanism in place to suit virtually everyone.

☒	Question	Why this matters
☐	7.3.10 Microsoft isn't running some of the courses I think we need – what other options do I have?	Microsoft has developed a set of learning partners that provide training on their product set. The courses they run, especially for new technologies are often subsidised by Microsoft and are available through the Partner Learning Centre.

7.4 Getting Some Support

Some of the areas provided on support are obvious, others less so. To begin with, core benefits associated with the various levels of the Partner Network clearly articulate the "gives" and "gets" of the partnership you are entering into. All of these can be found on the partner portal and are all described in detail and are laid out in clear areas with logical headings. Explore the portal homepage and you'll find:

- Information on licensing benefits (such as which software products you can use for free)
- Training benefits (training vouchers, courses available, events, webinars and podcasts)
- Marketing benefits (access to marketing materials, use of the Partner Network and product logos, pre-built demo's and pre-sales materials, use of Microsoft venue for events)
- Technical support (number of support incidents you get, who to call, how to request support)

There are other areas of support available and these will really relate to your area of specialisation and how much time and effort you put in to the relationship you have with Microsoft.

This section covers some of the core areas of support available, how you can access them, and what they can do for you. But for more depth information on everything you can take advantage of, as a result of your investment in Partner Network, get familiar with the portal. Make sure everyone in your company is subscribing to information and regularly visiting the areas of the partner portal that are relevant to their individual roles and areas of responsibility.

☒	Question	Why this matters
☐	7.4.1 Do I get any free technical support as a partner?	The level of support you receive is linked to the level of membership you have in the Partner Network. All partners have access to the Online Technical Communities. These are forums providing access to Microsoft engineers who will respond to your questions within a stated number of hours. Certified and Gold partners have access to pre-sales technical support, called Technical Sales Assistance. This service is delivered over the phone, and provides all the help you need to win a deal – from whitepapers, to data, to presentations. Gold partners, and partners with the ISV Competency, get access to a Microsoft technical consultant over the phone who can help with any technical issue, training or question you have.
☐	7.4.2 How do I know which support numbers I should call for my issue?	If you ever have any doubt about who to call – just call the Ask Partner support team, and they'll direct you to the right technical support team.
☐	7.4.3 When should I make the step from using the free support, to purchasing a support contract?	This decision is down to you – but usually you would decide to purchase support hours when it becomes business critical that you get immediate support. For smaller businesses, purchasing additional hours for the Technical Advisory Services (phone based) team should suffice – but for larger companies, or those working in areas where server-downtime is disastrous e.g. banks, you should seriously consider purchasing a Partner Advantage support contract (in-person).

☒	Question	Why this matters
☐	7.4.4 I'm finding Microsoft licensing a bit confusing. Are there any experts who can help me?	There is a licensing support line (which you get to by calling the Ask Partner support helpline) and these trained staff can answer simple or hard to find licensing questions. If they don't know the answer they will escalate the question to the right people globally. The more specific you can be about the question the more likely you are to get a resolution there and then. There is also an online tool which you can use to help you generate customer quotes for licensing, called LicenseWise.
☐	7.4.5 Should I contact my account manager when I have questions with my Partner Network membership?	It depends on the nature of your question, and the relationship you want to have with your account manager. You can use your account manager to get help, but you may want to focus your relationship on building your business. The best place to go really is the Ask Partner helpline.
☐	7.4.6 What is there beyond the Partner Network to support my customer engagements?	In addition to the benefits of belonging to the Partner Network, Microsoft also provides additional paid for services from the Partner Advantage support for incidents and training to 'Services Ready' which provides IP and best practice to help you to accelerate skills development within your organisation.
☐	7.4.7 How do I make sure I make the right decisions during the transition from Partner Programme to Partner Network?	First port of call is the Ask Partner helpline or your account manager. Microsoft are aware that there will be concerns and are allowing over twelve months for the migration and will be having a growing number of events that will explain what is going on. The safest bet is to make sure you keep up to date with new products, have happy customers and get your people qualified. These are the cornerstones of your involvement today and will be an even greater focus in the Partner Network.

☒	Question	Why this matters
☐	7.4.8 With all the Partner Network changes, what support can I get from Microsoft to help the migration?	This is a big change and Microsoft know that it will require a time and cost investment from partners to skill staff for the latest exams, updated marketing collateral and administer the membership account. Microsoft will be setting up a series of events over the coming year to keep you up to speed with all the changes, and these changes will also all be published on the partner portal. The Ask Partner helpline is the best place to go with your questions as they can answer everything from "when can I use the new logo?" to "how can I make sure I'm Advanced on day one?". (P.S. incase you were wondering, the answers to those questions are: Oct 2010, and look out for the Advanced requirements on the portal then start taking the new exams)
☐	7.4.9 Should I be committing R&D time to Microsoft's new products?	You need to decide how much you want to be on the bleeding edge. As a Microsoft partner your customers will have an expectation that you are up to date. However they may not need you to be delivering on the leading edge. In general, Microsoft like partners who get involved early, this helps to make the product better for launch and provides evidence of use – marketing opportunities to you.

☒	Question	Why this matters
☐	7.4.10 How much help does Microsoft offer if I decide to get involved at a beta stage with new products?	Short answer - lots. From both a business and technical perspective there are lots of programmes that will help you. In the business area there are opportunities for case studies, early adopter stories, inclusion in launch literature and even being invited to speak at events. Technically there are programmes such as TAP and Metro which offer early access to software, training and support. There are also opportunities to attend compatibility workshops or to test application scalability. Remember though that these resources are finite and Microsoft understandably wants to see your commitment as well as the customer opportunity. If your desire to be involved is driven by a large customer opportunity then this will help.
☐	7.4.11 How can I get support to understand the implications of new initiative such as BPOS and Windows Azure?	These are huge investment areas for Microsoft and hence they need partners to be involved to make them a success. There are regular events covering both technology and business aspects and at summary and in depth levels. If these are areas of interest to you then let people know (account manager first) as there are lots of programmes to encourage you to work with these offerings (Microsoft need success stories from partners to generate the virtuous circle of adoption)

☒	Question	Why this matters
☐	7.4.12 What help can I get to make sure I make the right architectural decisions when using Microsoft products?	Depending on your tier level you can request an "Architecture Design Session" (ADS). These give you access to Microsoft experts who will help you solve your current architectural design needs and also make sure that decisions you make today will be good in the future. There are also similar offerings that help with your business design needs called "Business Design Sessions" (BDS) – no surprise there! As always the greater the business opportunity that is driving your request the more likely you are to get one.

Chapter

8

Funny you should say that

Laughter gives us distance. It allows us to step back from an event, deal with it and then move on.

Bob Newhart (Comedian, 1929 –)

L IVING in the IT world we all come across the odd character or situation. The last Chapters of questions were valuable – but not very exciting or engaging. They could hardly be described as fun. What the book is missing are some stories or anecdotes which bring the Smart Questions to life.

Now life isn't always fun. Some of the stories are painful and expensive. But that makes them all the more valuable.

If we'd interspersed these stories with the questions it would have made the last Chapters too long. It would also have prevented you using the questions as checklists or aide-memoires. So we've grouped together our list of stories in this Chapter. I'm sure that you have your own stories – both positive and negative - so let us know them:

stories@Smart-Questions.com

Stories from the front line

Spot the difference!

We once had a customer who brought in two photographs of his computer (not the screen), one on a day he said it was working and one when it wasn't. He said "As a Microsoft Gold partner you should be able to diagnose the problem"

Where is my internet?

A large customer of ours for whom we supported the servers only complained to us that they didn't have internet access. Because they had organised their own internet service provider we didn't have any details and the person on their site who did was away for the weekend. After many phone calls and threats from the customer to leave us if we didn't sort out the problem we managed to trace the provider to BT and got to speak to someone there who was very helpful, they said "your customer hasn't paid the bill for 6 months so we have cut them off"

The satisfaction of our next phone call to the person in charge was worth every minute of dealing with this problem.

Anonymous

How do I print my voicemail?

Why won't you respond?

We are a Small Business Specialist and one of our customers who has his email on his own exchange server lost internet access for 4 days when his router failed. Eventually after losing all patience he phoned us up and threatened legal action after we hadn't responded to any of his email requests for help.

When we explained if he didn't have internet access the emails would be able to find their way to us he said "Google maps have a lot to answer for"

My Printer won't work

One of your engineers was here last week, he fitted a new monitor but now my printer won't work, it's saying out of ink! I want someone out here today and don't expect to have to pay for it as obviously your engineer broke it.

That's not my password!

I keep typing in my password and stars keep coming up, that's not my password, can you send me a new keyboard please.

There's a virus on my PC

We had one lady who wanted us to change some settings on her PC remotely so we talked her through allowing us to get remote access. As soon as we got control of her PC she started to panic on the phone, "My PC has a virus, it's moving all on its own" she shouted then immediately switched it off and unplugged it.

After a couple of minutes hesitation she came back to the phone and told us she would bring the PC to us to get the virus removed. It took a while but when we explained what she thought was a virus was us moving the mouse she calmed down. She still wanted to bring the PC in to us though because the mouse moving when she wasn't doing it was "spooky".

It's illegal

Customer: "It says I've performed an illegal operation and will be shut down. Have I done something wrong?"

Enter

You must have come across this one.

Engineer: "What does the screen say now?"
Customer: "It says, 'Hit ENTER when ready'."
Engineer: "Well?"
Customer: "How do I know when it's ready?"

Pictures

Engineer: "Which format are the images you send?"
Customer: "Rectangular, 15x11 centimetres."

Cannot access application

Customer: "I have just formatted my hard disk and now I don't seem to be able to access your application"

Case Study: Nimbus

"The work in the ADS is proving to be critical to the long term success of Nimbus and its clients."

N I M B U S

from strategy to reality

Ian Gotts, Chairman and CEO   *http://www.nimbuspartners.com*

 ### Things needed sorting

Nimbus Control is a business process management application which is used by organisations to capture, manage and deploy operational processes to their entire workforce. Microsoft Office SharePoint Server (MOSS2007) was becoming the default portal and document repository for enterprises and 70% of our clients had plans to deploy it. Therefore Nimbus Control needed to be tightly integrated into MOSS. But which areas of functionality, and what technical approach were critical decisions.

 ### Time for action

We could have gone back through the Partner Network and identified other partners who were experts at MOSS implementations. But we needed more than that. We needed the critical insights that only one of the Microsoft MOSS team would have. Insights not just about the current functionality, but also the product roadmap to future-proof our investment.

As an account-managed Gold Partner we were able to schedule an Architecture Design Session (ADS) where our architects could spend 2 days with the brightest and best in the Microsoft MOSS team. Together they designed the architecture for the integration, massively reducing the learning curve of the Nimbus team and giving them the confidence to develop the integration in-house rather than rely on expensive sub-contractors.

Life is looking better

The MOSS integration was developed in a few short weeks, rather than months of trial and error it would have taken without the ADS. The value was not just speed to market, but the confidence that the integration would scale to meet the needs of our enterprise customers who are deploying Nimbus Control inside MOSS to 100,000s of users. Finally, as MOSS2010 is being launched there is the knowledge that the integration was built in such as way that there is no need for a costly re-write.

Case Study: Technology Associates

"CSAT helps retain customers and win business, while avoiding the time and expense of developing or purchasing our own electronic survey system."

Kelvin Kirby, Director of the EPM Consulting Group, Technology Associates *http://www.techassoc.com*

 ## Things needed sorting

Despite developing a global reputation for excellence around Microsoft solutions and obtaining a client list that includes many Times Top 100 and Fortune 500 companies, the company has never been complacent. Measuring customer satisfaction was a foundation for benchmarking services and setting new targets. Traditionally, the business had approached customers directly with questionnaires to gather feedback after engagements. Ideally, it wanted to capture this data electronically, by creating an online survey system. However third party solutions were prohibitive in terms of cost and the time.

 ## Time for action

At a time when Technology Associates was finding it impossible to find the survey systems it needed, Microsoft launched its Customer Satisfaction (CSAT) Index. The service, available to Microsoft Certified Partners, is an online resource administered by TNS, a leading market research company. The Microsoft CSAT Index is easy to use and doesn't require much administration. It's fast and simple—and it provided the detailed insight into customer satisfaction levels that we needed.

Life is looking better

The Microsoft CSAT Index has contributed to Technology Associates winning new business. Using the insight gained from the surveys, the company can set carefully defined goals, which help build trusted relationships with customers. CSAT has helped to retain customers and win business, while avoiding the time and expense of developing or purchasing an electronic survey system.

Case Study: Contemporary plc

"We continually invest in our Microsoft partnership and it pays back in increased opportunities which strengthen our customer relationships and extend our market reach..."

The Business Intelligence People

Andy Steer, Managing Director

http://www.contemporary.co.uk

 ## Things needed sorting

We had been delivering Business Intelligence solutions for over fifteen years – and were keen to exploit the opportunity to develop the portion of our business that delivered solutions on the Microsoft platform. Although we were a Gold partner we hadn't really utilised our Microsoft contacts to gain insight and ideas about how we could differentiate ourselves in the market – based on their experience and knowledge of what was working with other partners in our space. We needed to have a constructive conversation with the right people within Microsoft so that we could develop our Microsoft business and increase what was fast becoming a key revenue stream for us.

 ## Time for action

We were fortunate to have an industry expert in the business who had identified a key market driver within the NHS and had worked with our marketing team to create a highly targeted proposition. Our partner account manager organised a meeting with the key people within the NHS business area of Microsoft who were incredibly helpful in extending what was already a sound idea. They suggested we looked at differentiating our proposition further by working with another partner from a completely different solution area who also had experience in the healthcare sector; their solution and skills fitted perfectly with our Business Intelligence capability and gave us a real WOW factor to go to market with.

Life is looking better

We made contact with the other partner the next day and met up with them within a week. We both quickly realised how compatible our two businesses were and how much opportunity there was for us to go to market together. Even more, we found an existing customer of ours who had already identified a need our new partner could fulfil – so a week after that we were meeting the customer together and putting forward some suggestions. Our customer loved it! We feel like we have really gained two new sound business partners here (one of which is Microsoft) and some additional resources that really enhance our core business.

Case Study: Brightstarr Ltd

"The benefits to us in being an active Microsoft partner and the effort that takes are not always obvious. What is obvious is the additional help we get when we ask for it, and the impact that has on the results we achieve."

Will Saville, Managing Director   *http://www.brightstarr.co.uk*

 ## Things needed sorting

We had recently completed a new project with Oxford Said Business School, where we had developed a rich, engaging website using Microsoft Office SharePoint Server and recognised we could well have identified a significant market opportunity. We had set aside marketing budget and identified our marketing partner to help us create a new pipeline of opportunities in the Higher Education sector but wanted to deliver a compelling event as a "Call to Action" for prospects to attend.

 ### Time for action

As a Microsoft Gold partner we knew we had the opportunity to book four customer events per year at Microsoft premises – and subsequently secured a room at Microsoft Cardinal Place to present to our qualified prospects. Our requirements for support however didn't stop there. We needed speakers from Microsoft to help us to drive home how valuable compelling websites are for Universities keen to attract the brightest students. Our Partner Account Manager and our marketing partner worked together to position the value of our event to the key people in the Higher Education sector at Microsoft and we were able to secure a top speaker to attend and present. Not only that but the marketing people for HE agreed to promote our event on the various blogs and twitter sites to help us drive attendance.

Life is looking better

The event is scheduled for 4th November 2009 and we can't wait! We have a really exciting agenda to deliver and some fantastic prospects coming along which will really drive the success of our marketing investment. We would never have been able to get this campaign to market quite as quickly or in such a meaningful way without the support we got as a result of being a Microsoft Gold partner.

Case Study: NCI Technologies

"Partnering is a 2 way process, the more you give the more you get. Partnering with Microsoft creates opportunities that incentivise your staff and solve problems for your customers."

Chris Penrose, Director   *http://www.nci-technologies.co.uk*

 ## Things needed sorting

As a fast growing company, employing staff that have knowledge and expertise in all the latest Microsoft software is difficult. Being based in Devon and Cornwall, training courses always meant travel and overnight stays, increasing the costs dramatically. In order to gain significant benefits for our customers and ourselves we needed to bring training on the core products in house. Budget, time and premises were all taken into account when seeking a resolution.

 ## Time for action

By using the certification processes we aimed at training staff to train our staff. The Microsoft learning resources, available as one of the benefits of being a Microsoft partner, are constantly updated. This allowed us to focus efforts on improving the quality of knowledge for our technical teams on new products and getting ahead of the game. We also needed to source the material for the trainer to present. Being a Gold Partner made this simple as we had access to the Official Microsoft training manuals.

Life is looking better

We now have a Microsoft Certified Trainer who can train our engineers in house at convenient dates on a variety of Microsoft software. He sources discounted exam vouchers when they are available and gets updates to the training manuals as they are delivered. The success of this has proven itself tenfold by reduced costs, better trained staff and time scheduling. We have also started to train our customers on supporting Microsoft technologies creating another source of income.

Funny you should say that

Chapter

And here is where we leave you ... for now anyway

A conclusion is the place where you got tired of thinking.

Albert Bloch (American Artist, 1882 – 1961)

A ND so finally we reach the end of what has been a truly enjoyable but mammoth task.

As we said right at the beginning, you have made a choice as a Microsoft partner to bet your business on Microsoft technology – which must mean you do see the value in delivering solutions on the platform. You must be reasonably confident that you can commercially succeed and develop your business with Microsoft as your chosen vendor. Hopefully you now have a better idea as to how you really can maximise your investment as a Microsoft partner.

If there are just three things that you take away from this book, let it be these:

1. Put in the time and effort to understand yourself and your business opportunity
2. Engage with the Partner Network – making sure you have a clear goal for your reason to be part of it, understanding exactly what you need from it, spending time finding what you need and then using it!

3. Finally, don't expect Microsoft to run your business for you. It's a two-way partnership – put in effort, and you'll get a great return

The Partner Network is there to help you accelerate your success – sounds a bit cheesy – but then we all like a bit of cheese now and again don't we?

Appendix – Partner Network References

There were a lot of references to tools on the partner portal, or numbers you should call. We could leave you to find all the resources yourself, but as you've read the entire book it seems only fair that we point you in the right direction...

Useful Telephone Numbers

Service	What's it for?	Telephone
Ask Partner	Ask about: to-customer licensing, product questions, accessing technical support	0844 800 6006
Regional Service Centre	Ask about: any Partner Network questions, internal-use licences, membership renewal, portal access issues	0800 917 3128

Useful Web Links

Resource	What's it for?	URL
Partner Portal	The hub for partner tools and resources	*www.microsoft.com/uk/partner*
BizSpark	A programme for software start-ups	*www.microsoft.com/bizspark*
Channel Builder	Connect with other partners	*www.microsoft.com/uk/partner/channelbuilder*
CSAT Index	Customer satisfaction survey tool	*www.microsoft.com/uk/partner/csat*
Demo Showcase	Access pre-built Microsoft demos	*http://demoshowcasesuite.com/*
Digital Content	Get Microsoft	*https://partner.microsoft.*

Resource	What's it for?	URL
Direct	product information embedded in your website	*com/UK/40083773*
Digital Distribution	Site to download internal-use licences and view your licence statement	*https://www.microsoft.co m/msppdd/*
Empower for ISVs	Programme for ISV partners offering development support and software licenses	*www.microsoft.com/uk/p artner/empower*
Kickstart Videos	A series of training videos to help you understand the Partner Network	*www.microsoft.com/uk/p artner/kickstart*
Learning Paths	Suggested training paths to help you understand which courses to take	*www.microsoft.com/uk/p artner/learningpaths*
LicenseWise	Online tool to help you configure customer licensing quotes	*http://www.microsoft.co m/licensing/licensewise/*
Logo Builder	Access your Microsoft partner logos	*www.microsoft.com/uk/p artner/logo*
Microsoft Action Pack	Programme for Registered partners offering Internal-use licenses and sales resources	*www.microsoft.com/uk/p artner/maps*
Microsoft Club	Rebate programme for resellers and system builders	*https://microsoftclub.mic rosoft.com*
Microsoft Partner Community	Informally network online with partners and Microsoft	*http://www.microsoftpart nercommunity.co.uk*
Microsoft Sales	Product 'bible' to	*www.microsoft.com/uk/p*

Resource	What's it for?	URL
Toolkit	give to your sales teams	*artner/gearup*
Microsoft Toolkits (TX)	Pre-built, high quality Microsoft presentations	*http://www.microsofttoolkits.co.uk*
Online Technical Communities	Online technical forums	*www.microsoft.com/uk/partner/technicalsupport*
Partner Events	Run your own event at Microsoft for your customers	*www.microsoft.com/uk/partner/events*
Partner Learning Centre	Hub for training courses and materials	*www.microsoft.com/uk/partner/plc*
Partner Marketing Centre	Hub for marketing resources and information	*https://www.partnermarketingcenter.com/*
Partner Newsletter	The key resource for receiving information from Microsoft	*www.microsoft.com/uk/partner/newsletter*
Partner Sales Resources	Hub for sales resources and information	*http://www.partnersalesresources.com*
Photo Library	Stock imagery for you to use	*www.microsoft.com/uk/partner/salesmarketing*
Pinpoint	Customer search tool to find partners	*http://pinpoint.microsoft.com/*
Product Images	Product boxshots for you to use	*www.microsoft.com/uk/partner/salesmarketing*
RSS Feeds	Get the latest information by RSS	*www.microsoft.com/uk/partner/rss*
Solution Profiler	Profiling your company for sales leads	*www.microsoft.com/uk/partner/profiler*
Technical Advisory Services	Telephone consultancy	*www.microsoft.com/uk/partner/technicalsupport*
Technical Sales Assistance	Telephone pre-sales competitive support	*www.microsoft.com/uk/partner/technicalsupport*

Notes pages